Life Skills

for the

GW00542532

Ne..
Millennium

Creating a New, Joyful Life

by Paula Sunray, Ph.D.

© Copyright 1999 Paula Sunray.

ISBN 1-892745-21-6 (Electronic Book)
ISBN 1-892745-22-4 (Print Book)

Printed in the United States of America

For information on Petals of Life, please contact the publisher at:

MDJ, Inc./Petals of Life
231 Oil Well Road, Suite C, Jackson, TN 38305
(901) 668-6622, (901) 664-2743 Fax
petals@petalsoflife.com
http://www.petalsoflife.com/

This book is dedicated to Caroline Myss, who has inspired me in so many ways.

--Paula Sunray

Foreword

In the first decade of the New Millennium, different tools are needed, and an entirely new approach to education. As we embrace the new reality of a world composed more of thought than substance, we must begin to rethink the basis of that reality.

Dr. Sunray is one of the few old masters who has the knowledge and connection to the higher realms necessary for the journey ahead--the journey of the mind into the final frontier. Her instruction is "akami," channeled from the highest dimension. Her method is playful and reminiscent of friends around a campfire from long ago.

Let the master come down from the podium and empower you with her gifts of sharing. Begin the journey into the final frontier. Begin to know who you are.

Pila of Hawaii
"Seer" and Teacher of the Ancient Wisdom

Endorsements

"There are teachers who are new to the great change upon us and capitalize on the fear and anxiety it produces, and then there are the Old Ones--the Old Souls who have stood on the high mountain. Dr. Sunray is one such teacher-- a Wise One who has returned to help in the time of greatest need."

--Pila of Hawaii, "Seer" and author of <u>The Secrets and Mysteries of Hawaii</u>

"*Life Skills for the New Millennium* is a book not to be missed. It is new, different, unique, chock full of thought-provoking definitions and perspectives on a host of spiritual concepts, and offers a provocative new definition of "enlightenment.".

Dr. Sunray includes powerful exercises that produce dramatic results, and paints a vivid and inspiring portrait of the spiritual master that is practical and achievable by the ordinary reader.

Challenging both convention and our habitual patterns of thinking, Paula Sunray offers an adventure unlike anything now in print. She recognizes the great transition underway on our planet now and how individual responsibility and empowerment will be keys to our navigating the future successfully. This is a life-transforming book."

---Susan E. Mehrtens, Ph.D., Yale

"I like it! We can all profit from reading this insightful book. It feels right!"

--Ruth Montgomery, author of "Strangers Among Us" & "The World To Come: Guidance For A Coming Age"

5

" Rev. Paula Sunray has written an insightful book that I highly recommend to everyone interested in developing a practical approach to active interchange."

---Caroline Myss, author of Why People Don't Heal and Anatomy of the Spirit

"Paula Sunray's book *Life Skills for the New Millennium* is a precious guide for people in search of their true potentiality. It offers our modern society the wisdom previously shared by the druids, shamans, and other guides who were able to move between the visible and invisible realities. Dr. Sunray openly shares her evolution of thoughts and truth with clarity and a deep confidence in the ability of human beings to come home to their full awareness. This book is a great source of inspiration and encouragement to anyone interested in full living."

--Anja Kulovesi, author of "Daily Life Magic," Finland

"Paula Sunray is one of the most important guides into the next century. This is the course of courses. Paula points the way into the next century. It's dynamic, refreshing, thought-provoking."

--Rev. Sandi Shore, Ms.D, author of the "Sandbox" collection

"Life Skills for the New Millennium will change your life. I highly recommend it."

--Kathryn Harwig, author of "The Millennium Effect"

Table of Contents

7

Exercises

Acknowledgments

This little book is the culmination of years of study and the search for truth. I have had so many wonderful teachers that it is impossible to name them all. I can only say that my best teachers were those who challenged me the most.

My greatest thanks go to Sheradon Bryce and her important channeling work on this planet, and to all the teachers, physical and non-physical, who have inspired me and stretched me spiritually, mentally, and emotionally: Seth, Cayce, Ramtha, Lazaris, Kryon, Bashar, Serge King, Caroline Myss, and a host of others. Many of their teachings thread their way through this book. May they be as inspiring to you as they were to me.

I also wish to thank Michele Janine Johnson for believing in this book, and Sheila Shay, Joyce Ferenc, Jan Ferenc, Pat Dix, Joe Townend, Florence Andre, and Candace Woods for their invaluable skills and help in my work as Director of the National Interfaith Seminary.

My dear friends, Pila, Merle, Lynne, and Patty have loved and supported me through many a rough time. I thank them from the bottom of my heart. And perhaps, even most of all, I thank my students and clients who have contributed the greatest joy to my life.

INTRODUCTION

This book is a spiritual exercise and is not written to instruct or indoctrinate. I have simply chosen to write what I have learned in the last 15 years as I have searched for spiritual truth. What I have learned is not necessarily what I believe, because my beliefs change almost daily. I am in process, and I am continually challenged by new concepts as I go along.

I have learned that nothing is written in cement and that no belief is worth arguing over or fighting about, because we all have a limited view of the higher perspective. We can never fully know the big picture while we are on this limited earth plane.

Seventeen years ago I began a journey and a labor of love. I decided that I must have the answers to the questions: "Where am I from, how did I get here, why am I here, and where am I going?" In other words, I wanted to know precisely what I was supposed to be doing and learning in this lifetime.

I wanted an answer to all the metaphysical questions such as "Who and what is God? Is there life after death? Is there any purpose to this lifetime? Why is there suffering? What exists apart from earth life?"

I set out methodically to find the answers, and I decided that the best way to learn it was to "teach" it. I had been a professional musician and university teacher for many years, and had learned that the more I taught, the better musician I became. I applied the same idea to metaphysics.

As soon as I made it clear to the heavens that I wanted to learn everything possible, Spirit immediately took over and presented me with a variety of lessons and challenges. It became clear to me that there were some basic Universal Laws at work.

I could see that my perceptions and responses to life were like boomerangs that flew back in my face over and over. I could see that life changed according to the way I framed it. I noticed that fears caused depression and that knowledge and enlightenment resulted in empowerment.

As I learned and applied my new understandings, I began to teach classes about basic Universal Truths. The students also began to feel less fearful and more empowered, and I could see the relationship between our belief systems and our experiences in life.

At first, I took my teacher role seriously and thought that I was a very good teacher. As time passed, I realized that I was learning as much from the students as they were learning from me. I came to truly know that we are teacher and student to each other, and that knowledge is not the same as wisdom. One need not ever read a book to be "wise." In fact, too much knowledge can sometimes distract us from the basics of truth.

My concept of truth has changed through the years from the grand and universal truths to the basic and simple truths of everyday life.

Each day I struggle with my issues, and each and every day I struggle with the pain and triumphs of being human and vulnerable, but I find that I am struggling less, and little by little I am learning to be a happier and more joyful being.

As I learn more and try to "walk my talk," I find that I don't fit comfortably with any of the present earth systems. The time comes for all of us to leave the tribe and the community and become our own person, independent of tribal beliefs. This can be a challenging time and it may feel lonely for awhile, but I believe that it is a necessary step toward walking the realms of higher consciousness.

I did not write this book to be popular. Some of you will be shaken by some of the things I say and perhaps even angry. I'm not writing this book to upset you. I'm writing it because my own spirit started pouring out its heart and insisted upon being heard.

In a way, this book is for the brave and courageous - the truth seekers who care more about truth than what the neighbors think.

You will see that I am not some enlightened person telling you what to believe. Quite the contrary, I am a struggling student of life who has great immaturity in some respects and great empowerment in others.

I hope that you will have fun with this book and not take it too seriously. This is not life and death material, it is life and _life_ material. If there is a purpose to this book, it would be to encourage you to love and enjoy your life no matter what you think and believe; to learn and grow according to your own choices and preferences. As my friend Philip would say, "Go in peace so you won't be in pieces."

Paula Sunray

CHAPTER ONE

Beware of Truth Controllers

Don't be a truth seeker. Be a truth finder.

I have spent many years, many hours, and many dollars in my search for spirituality. What is a truth seeker? A truth seeker is a person who cares about the quality of their existence and wants to know how to satisfy their incessant inner urge toward growth.

Who are truth controllers? They are people, institutions, systems, and hierarchies who want to keep people "little" so they can be "bigger." They want us to believe in the concept of good and bad, right and wrong, superior and inferior.

I have spent much of my life as a truth seeker, and although it was supremely exciting at times, it didn't lead to the pot at the end of the rainbow. It wasn't until I stood still and looked down at my own feet that I found the pot of gold. Today I am no longer a truth seeker, I am a truth <u>finder</u>.

I find truth in the present moment in everyday situations and experiences. I feel that the religions and spirituality of both the Old Age and the New Age have missed the mark because they are "seeking" schools who teach that what you are looking for is far away and difficult to attain. In other words, you can never be perfect enough or good enough. It is like the horse trying to eat the carrot that is suspended from its hat. The carrot is always in front and unattainable. You always feel like you aren't quite there yet.

I think it is time to grab the carrot and munch on it,

14

relish and enjoy it. The carrot is an ordinary vegetable - nothing fancy about it, yet it is extremely nutritious and is even known to have healing powers in the treatment of cancer and other illnesses.

The carrot could be called our spirituality. Spirituality is an everyday thing, and it also has great healing power. Truth seekers would want the carrot to be bathed in golden light. Truth controllers would tell you that you must study gardening and learn how to plant the seeds in the right directions at the right time astrologically and to chant the appropriate mantra. And after all that, you have to wait until they grow and are ripe for the picking.

Well, my friends, I think you've been had. You've been cheated, scolded, coerced, judged, blamed, and misled long enough. I think it is time to recognize that spirituality (the carrot) is an everyday thing and is present at all times and you don't have to do a thing to earn it or deserve it. Deity is life and life is deity.

How many days did you have this week that were fun, exciting, fulfilling, and radiant? How much passion for life did you feel this week? How much joy did you experience? If this was not an inspiring and exciting week for you, then ask yourself, "Why not?" If you are not filled with joy on a daily basis something has gone wrong somewhere. Something is not right. Something isn't working. What is it?

For my part, I notice a difference when I live out of my "low self" instead of my "high self." Churches have fed us half-truths and have hidden true teachings. We are all victims of amnesia. We have forgotten who we are.

We can trace it back to a time in history when there

were power struggles between the church and the common people. The churches and governments established systems of hierarchy in order to control the people. We lost our Godhood when we began to let others make decisions for us, when we began to let others lead us and control us. Our demise came when we gave away our own power and let others assume a position of superiority over us.

It is not necessary to linger on the past. It is simply time to rectify the errors and head back to a saner reality. Now is the moment that counts, and now is the time to take back our equality and Godhood and return to a state of truth.

CHAPTER TWO

The World is Made Up

"You are the eye through which God sees."
-author unknown

Not much of what we have been taught is true. The systems and rules here have all been made up, and we take them much too seriously. If we could truly see it as a story we have made up and enjoy it as a story, we would be better off. At some point, we will have to stand back and detach from the world of illusion, otherwise we will get carried away with the trauma and drama of the "movie."

Being emotionally attached to the movie causes unnecessary pain. When we step back, our core essence can observe without identifying with the illusion. It can step out of the movie and become real on its own, making its own decisions without having to follow the plot of the movie.

The only thing that matters, ultimately, is associating with the truth. The truth can only be found "within," where the God-awareness resides. It is our God-awareness that observes life. This is our true self. The personality self is the false self which thinks the movie is the real world.

Our mind/body is a vessel and we can fill it with whatever we choose. We can fill it with fear and insecurity (the movie), or we can fill it with love, peace, and harmony (the observer true self).

There is no point to self-healing or meditation if we consider them to be the final goal. After we experience the inner peace of self-healing and meditation, we must then go a step further and feel the presence and feeling of God within. We must feel the awareness of God flowing through us and seeing through us as It experiences Its creations first hand.

The personality, or low self, thinks it is separate from God, but the high self, or God awareness, flowing through us cannot perceive separation. God awareness is like a vast ocean of "beingness" that expresses individually as waves. Each wave is separate even though it is one with the ocean. When we flow within ourselves, we are the ocean, and when we go outward to the edge of consciousness, we are the wave.

CHAPTER THREE

Exploring Feelings and Emotions

In order to live life at its fullest,
you must be able to process
your feelings and emotions.

In order to explore the ocean and be one with it, we need to dive in and experience it first hand. We can look at many pictures of the ocean, but that is not the same as experiencing it.

The same is true for the high self world. In order to know it, we must explore it, taste it, and <u>feel</u> it. How can we be a high self when we keep ourselves distanced from it?

The high self does not live from a point of view of fear. It lives from a point of view of courage, truth, honesty, feeling, and expression without guilt. It knows it's essence and honors it. It knows who it is, it is fully aware, and it understands. It sees everything from a higher perspective. The high self knows that it is a creator and not a victim. It knows that it creates its own experiences because it is a creator.

In order to understand feelings and emotions, we must go into them and experience them. Once we are one with a feeling, we are in charge of it. We can decide to keep the feeling, change it, or shift it.

We are in charge of energy. Emotion is really just repressed feeling. There is only one feeling in the universe and it is a happy, joyful energy. Whenever we get in touch with the true energy within and experience it without guilt, it will always be a grand feeling of joy.

To be a master of our energy, we need to be <u>aware.</u> We need to go into our body and experience our feelings and emotions in order to be aware of them. How do they feel? What is their size and shape? How big are they? What are they made of?

Just as we explore an ocean, it is the awareness that makes the master. As creators, once we know the size, shape, and content of something, we can change it if we want to. Just as a shaman does, we can "shape-shift" and change our fears into pleasures.

We can easily change fear into excitement. They feel very similar. We can change anger into passion. We can choose what we want to feel and create that experience right now.

With awareness, we can process and understand. By processing, we ask a lot of questions and we answer them very honestly as we explore deeper and deeper into the ocean of ourselves. Once we have explored it and experienced it, then we have healed it. Because we have healed it, we will begin to enjoy the process and feel the empowerment of creation.

Consciousness and Guilt

We all live out of guilt much more than we realize. All of our negativity and suffering comes from repeating thoughts over and over in our heads. These thoughts come from our low self and they are mostly guilt-based.

The low self is a creator of emotion (repressed feeling). Emotion is the same thing as consciousness. Emotion, consciousness, and guilt are all very similar. When we die, we will not take our consciousness with us.

Consciousness (the collective emotions of guilt, worry, fear, and stress) is the glue that is holding us together mentally until we get our act together and move out of ego. When we are able to live life with intensity, passion, knowledge, and feeling, we won't need consciousness anymore.

Notice that consciousness is not the same as knowledge. Consciousness is ego-based and is a product of the low self. Knowledge, feeling, and life are high self attributes. Guilt is "emotion" based and knowledge is "feeling" based.

We will live in consciousness until we get sick and tired of it, and then we will work our way out of the restrictive cocoon, and become a butterfly who flies with feeling and passion. Feeling is the same as intensity and intensity is the same thing as knowledge. Knowledge is the same as life and feeling, etc.. It is all the same thing.

The only game we have going here is the choice to play with emotion or feeling. In order to choose feeling, we must have a SELF first - a self that knows itself, honors itself, and is true to itself. Only a true self is free enough to feel FEELING and express it in all that it does. Only a true self knows how to love and have fun.

CHAPTER FOUR

The Core Essential Self

If you give up the fear of the ego
and follow your core essence,
you can never go wrong.

When it comes right down to it, the cause of most of our problems is the loss of contact with our true essential self. When we were born it was intact, but as we grew up, we took on the identity of the personality and lost the essence of SELF.

When this connection is lost it feels like something is missing. This absence gives us a "Swiss cheese" self, and we try to fill in the gaps with addictions, relationships, and any fillers we can find. The filler part of us is our "personality" which has false ideas and beliefs based on the external world (the movie). We will never be able to fill the holes using our personality self.

What is missing is contact with our true essence - our essential self. Essence is our true nature. It is our high self or impersonal self. That essence is like the sun shining at our center with a radiance and brilliance that is covered with the shadows and negativity of our false, low self personality.

Many people have tried to reconnect with their true inner self by meditating, praying, or studying. Although they are partially successful, they have missed a crucial function - that of identifying and healing the outer ego personality that keeps them stuck in fear and insecurity.

The only way we can relieve and release our inner

conflicts is by using the psychological methods of inquiry and awareness. We can only get to our spiritual self by addressing the personality issues that block us from our inner essential self. Psychological work is inseparable from spiritual work.

Most people do not like the drudgery of self-work. They do not have the willingness or patience to do the hard work. It is my contention that the spiritual work cannot be done without the psychological confrontation of our ego issues.

Most people walk around with dead and numbed emotional systems. They have a wall of denials around their issues. Most people have lost their capacity for depth of emotion because of their fear of vulnerability, fear of feeling, and a host of other reasons.

Many people deaden their bodies with addictive substances and blocked emotions. No wonder they feel cut off from their "essence." Essence is not experienced in the mind, it is experienced in the body.

When we deaden our bodies we are cut off from the inner radiation of love, joy, and happiness from our core self. The spiritual road must include a reconnection with, and an appreciation for, the body - a reunion of body and spirit.

Instead of rehashing the past like traditional psychotherapy, we need to be free of the past. We need to heal our wounds and free our resentments so that we can experience the joy of the moment and the spontaneity of life in the present.

We have a strength and joy at our center that is seldom experienced. To really be in our essence, we need to know who we really are and act accordingly. Our true self has a strong longing for truth and healing and will lead us in the right direction. If we give up the fear of the ego and follow our core essence, we will never be wrong.

CHAPTER FIVE

The Low Self and the High Self

Your beliefs and behaviors change,
but your worth never changes.

Along the way we lost parts of ourselves and we have never regained them because we don't really know who we are. We don't really understand what our makeup is, and we don't have a clear idea of where we are going.

One of the things that confuses us the most is the conflicting inner voices we hear. Just as we are on the way to achieving our dreams, an inner voice begins to whisper negative and deflating things in our ears. Think about how many times you have been excited about something and you suddenly lost your inspiration. This is what we call the eternal conflict between low self and high self. We need to understand this conflict if we want to achieve our dreams and find the pot at the end of the rainbow.

The <u>low</u> self is the part of us that allows itself to be limited by listening to others instead of trusting itself. It is the part that only sees small pieces of things and not the whole. It is the part that is fearful and afraid and never takes risks. It is the part of us that thinks that power and goodness and miracles are outside of itself.

The <u>high</u> self is the unlimited self that flows through us and guides us with its wisdom and love. It sees the whole because it comes from a higher perspective. It is a self of courage and propels us toward growth and risk taking. It is the part of us that recognizes our magnificence and worth and uses its loving power to create miracles every day.

The low self is the ego and the high self is the True Self. The low self is the self that whispers the negative and discouraging things in our ears, and the high self is the part that supports and encourages and guides us toward our highest good.

Most of our difficulties began when we got cut off from our high self, our spirit. We forgot that we are a spirit having a human life in order to learn from experience in a human body. We are <u>not</u> just a human who happens to have a spirit. We are a spirit who temporarily chooses to be in a human body.

Why did we come here? We came here to become more of who we are so that we will be more when we go back home to the heart of our Creator Source. In this way, our Creator continues to expand and become more and more.

How do we become more and more? By experiencing as many things as possible. There are no bad experiences - just <u>events</u> to experience. There is no such thing as a crisis - only an event.

The big problem is that most people are stuck in their low self, fearful of taking risks, and trying desperately to be good and noble at all times because that is what their religion taught them. Most people are not living life, they are living <u>hell</u>.

I don't believe that any of us ever intended to get stuck in this dilemma, and I don't believe that we ever wanted to diminish our life vibrancy each year of our life. Somehow we bought the false illusion, the sham, the farce. It was passed on to us by our parents, teachers, and institutions. It is all we have ever known.

26

Well, my dear friends, get ready to fly! We are going on an adventure together, and we are going to start with the only adventure there ever is - the journey back to the SELF, which is the residence of love and esteem, power and hope.

Whatever happened to our self-love and self-worth? It got very small when we gave away our power and started to listen to and rely on others. I invite you to take back your power NOW.

It's not really as hard as you think. All you have to do is remind yourself that you have two basic selves. One is afraid and listens only to what other people think, and the other is the spirit within that knows and understands all things from a higher perspective. It is courageous, loving, helpful, and wise.

The high self within is where all the self-love and esteem is - where all the support and encouragement is. The low self is the part that experiences fear, anxiety, limitation, judgment and defensiveness, while the high self is the part that experiences love, compassion, inspiration, unlimitedness, and creativity.

Self-love is a feeling of warmth and love toward our self. This is the natural feeling state of the high self. We will never find it in the lower self. Self-esteem does not have to do with what we do or achieve. It is a feeling of "beingness." It is a feeling of liking and accepting ourselves exactly as we are.

The real truth is that our worth never changes. Our beliefs and behaviors change, but our worth never changes. We are made of the same substance as our Creator. The son or daughter of a King doesn't have to do anything to be of worth. They are royalty at birth. We are sons and daughters of the ultimate King Creator.

The high self is the part of us that is born of royalty. We don't have to do anything special to inherit the kingdom.

When we begin to identify with the high self instead of the low self, we will begin to re-experience self-love because the energy of the high self IS love. We simply have to keep our radio station tuned to HHHS instead of LLLS.

That doesn't mean that we ever reject the low self and tell it to get lost. The low self is not unlovable, it is just little and afraid. We bring it along with us wherever we go, holding its hand so it won't feel afraid, while we follow the guidance of our parent high self.

The point of this whole explanation is that we must return to the spirit within if we want to return to sanity and true enlightenment.

It is the high self that has the impetus toward growth. It knows our purpose and the direction to take. It knows everything about us, because it travels with us from lifetime to lifetime. It is our real and true self. We must recover this true self if we are going to have authentic experiences which lead to growth and understanding. Our problems began when we lost touch with the high self and believed that the low self was all there was.

LOW SELF	HIGH SELF
The External World	Inner Wisdom
The Ego	The True Self
Judgmental	Compassionate
Fearful	Loving
Limited	Unlimited
Anxious	Peaceful
Feels Separate	Feels Connected
Defensive	Trusting
Closed	Open
Rationalization	Intuition
Contrived	Spontaneous
Acid	Alkaline
Emotion	Feeling
Lack	Abundance
Guilt	Joy
Thinking	Feeling
Control	Surrender
Self-Criticism	Self-Validation
Complaint	Gratitude

CHAPTER SIX

Intuition: The Voice of the High Self

The only true guide
that you will ever have
is your high self.

In order to live the truth of the high self, we must listen to the voice of the high self, which is speaking to us twenty-four hours a day. All we have to do is tune in.

We commonly call this voice "intuition." Intuition is a nebulous thing to many people. Many a husband shakes his head when his wife says, "Honey, I just get this feeling I shouldn't go to the party tonight" or "Robert, you've got to check the furnace today. I have a feeling that something isn't right."

Intuition is indeed a feminine attribute, but men have it also because we are all a mixture of feminine and masculine energies. We are basically androgenous, with both male and female polarities.

Webster's dictionary describes intuition as "the power of knowing," and that is precisely what intuition is: a power. We must learn to use this power of knowing if we want to live an authentic life in pursuit of authentic goals.

The voice of the high self is a gentle and kindly voice. It is quiet and calm, supportive and helpful. It speaks in quiet, simple language and always has our highest good in mind. It is very different from the voice of the ego which is judgmental, critical, and boastful.

The quality of our everyday life changes dramatically when we listen to the voice of the high self instead of the low self. All we have to do is listen to our gut feelings and follow our hunches.

Remember that intuition comes from within and speaks <u>through</u> you, like someone talking inside of you. It might help to think of the high self as a person or "being" that you can visualize when you close your eyes. You don't have to literally "see" it, you can just sense or perceive it.

For those of you who want to open more to your spiritual self and expand your spirituality, the only true guide that you will ever have is your high self. It is important, then, to trust this aspect of yourself, learn to slow down and calm down, and go inside and listen. Eventually, you will be able to sense and feel this guidance in all that you do.

CHAPTER SEVEN

Dropping the Illusions

*The first illusion that you must drop
is that there is a good and a bad.*

Now that you are armed with your high self as a guide, you are ready to take a look around you and see life through the eyes of your true self. You are still flesh and ego, but you now see the world through the eyes of the high self. You are ready to drop the old illusions, one at a time.

The old illusions have been hypnotized into us since the day we were born. We have been trained like a circus seal to respond at command without understanding what we are doing and why. We have been trained to think through the mind of the low self (the rational or conscious mind) instead of through the mind of the high self (the super-conscious mind).

Remember, the voice of the high self (intuition) comes to us and through us rather than being generated by us. We have to break the hypnotic spell of our parents and teachers and let the world speak to us in a new and magical voice.

The Illusion of Good and Bad

The first illusion we must drop is the idea of good and bad, right and wrong. The greatest damage has come from this illusion because it makes us feel unworthy and guilty. No wonder so many people walk around hanging their heads with shame, feeling heavy in their hearts.

Since most religions teach the concept of right and wrong, people have lost their spontaneity and spark of life trying to be good and proper. They suppress and repress their true feelings, and become more and more "dead" with each passing year.

The more we pretend to be "together," the more we miss the chance to grow and heal ourselves. Whoever or whatever taught us that we must be perfect to be spiritual or that we must be perfect before God will love us, ought to be strung up by the "can'ts" - I mean pants.

We don't need to be perfect; we need to be "real." We need to just be ourselves as we are, experiencing and responding according to our present state of consciousness. Nothing more is required to be spiritual - just "realness."

A spiritual teacher ought to model "life" and not perfection. A teacher needs to demonstrate realness, honesty, spontaneity, creativity, and the ability to take risks. Many so-called spiritual people, pretending to come from higher and better versions of spirituality, are really acting from the ego's need to feel better than everyone else.

Real spirituality is a direct experience in the now and is in constant flux. Life just "is" and we can respond to it any way we choose, although we must take responsibility for our response. When we refuse to be responsible for our life and ask others (our governments and churches) to make the rules for us, we must not then complain about the laws and the rules.

Many changes are about to happen on our planet and if we don't take back our responsibility in these coming years, we will lose more and more of our rights. We can no longer sit on the fence and live our lives by default, we must take a stand one way or the other.

The Illusion of Light and Dark

Another illusion is that light is good and dark is evil. Everything in this universe is made out of the same stuff, and that swirling mixture of stuff is love, joy, harmony, beauty, and life. We cannot see past a certain frequency of light. As the frequency of light gets higher and higher, it appears to get darker and darker to us because we can no longer see it with our eyes.

If you took a piece of clay and broke it in half and molded an angel from one piece and a devil from the other piece, would one be bad and the other good? No, they are both the same thing - a piece of clay, one and the same.

There is nothing evil or bad in this universe. The demons and the monsters are only our own thoughts scaring us to death. We are good at terrorizing ourselves with our thoughts. If we think something negative enough times it will form into a dense energy and seem very real to us. It lingers in our energy field and scares us in our dreams and also when we leave our body at death.

We have many of these monster thoughts around us from many years of fearful thinking, and we meet up with these "monsters" after we die. This "river of hell" around us is the Hell that the Bible speaks of, but it is not a devil or Satan that we meet, it is a mixture of the demons and monsters we have created in our own heads.

Does this make us bad people? Absolutely not. It makes us people who need to clear our energy fields of the old patterns of beliefs and attitudes. We can do that if we step out of the fearful negative mind of the ego (low self) and into the loving mind of the high self.

We can also learn to love our monsters. When you think of it, they are really quite pathetic and comical. They look so menacing and frightening, but if we just walk up to them, look them in the eye, and kiss them on the nose, they will vanish in a moment or transform themselves before our very eyes.

One night, as I was falling asleep, a very large monster face with beady, dark, menacing eyes, appeared before me. It looked straight at me. Its face had many folds of skin and was quite ugly.

I invited it to come closer, to come inside of me so I could experience it. I let it consume me and I consumed it. It was a bit unnerving, but it wasn't at all as bad as I thought it would be. Something very loving happened. Something very special passed between us, the face smiled, and then disappeared into nothingness.

That face was an aspect of myself that I needed to learn to love. It was a face created by my past fears and frights. One way or the other, we must each face our shadows and make friends with the dark.

CHAPTER EIGHT

Exploring the "Shadow"

The shadow is simply
an unexplored part of yourself.

The word "shadow" originated with Carl Jung, the famed analytical psychologist. According to Jung, it is critically important to accept and integrate the shadow side of us into our personality if we want to live rich and fulfilling lives.

There is nothing good or bad about the shadow. It is simply an unexplored part of ourselves. It is the part that we would rather keep hidden. It is the part that we won't let ourselves see because we think it is "bad."

Every time you reject a part of yourself, that part will become a disowned self that lives within you. We all have many disowned selves, and as long as we carry that energy within us, we will attract that same energy to us. Life will continually bring us face to face with the people who symbolize our disowned selves until we claim them and heal them.

There is nothing bad about the shadow self. It is simply an unknown part of ourselves that we have resisted exploring because of the connotations we have put upon it. Because the shadow is a vital, passionate, rich source of creativity and spontaneity, it is important to learn to open to this part of ourselves.

I think of the shadow as a hidden "altered" ego who lies buried deep within each one of us and is filled with pain, fear, or deep remorse. This pain or fear is so great that it must go deep enough to be completely hidden within the recesses of our being so that we are no longer even aware of it. Most of our blocks and limitations are a result of this hidden shadow self.

An Exercise to Bring the Shadow Into the Light

By answering the following questions in a rapid fire manner, without hesitating between sentences, you can trick the altered personality to come up and be healed:

1. "I hate the universe because _____."
Keep repeating and answering this question with anything that comes to your mind without stopping to think of your answers. Really FEEL the charge of the word "hate" as you answer the question. Keep answering at a rapid pace even if the answers have no meaning. Do this until an intense emotion begins to arise and express itself. Continue until the feeling has been discharged.

2. Now change the sentence to "I love the universe because _____."
Just as you did before, answer the questions in a rapid fire way. Really FEEL the word love as you repeat the sentences. If you cannot think of an answer, just keep repeating the sentence until an answer erupts. There should be no silence between the sentences.

The Illusion of Good and Bad Feelings

One of our illusions is that some of our feelings are good and some are bad. Let's re-examine this idea and redefine it according to the truth of this universe.

All things in the universe are simply energy expressing or <u>not</u> expressing. We can express the energy within us or we can suppress it or repress it. All energy is the same. Our entire universe is made of the same energy. New Agers call it "love." It is a <u>feeling</u>. It flows throughout the universe and throughout each of us. It is what we are made of. It is love.

We can either let this energy flow and express, or we can sit on it and hold it back. It is like watering the lawn with a garden hose. We can let the water flow as we water the garden, or we can crimp the hose and stop the water from coming out the nozzle.

When we let our feelings flow naturally, we are watering and nourishing ourselves and our lives, but when we sit on our feelings, we are blocking and deadening parts of ourselves. A positive emotion is <u>any</u> emotion that is owned and expressed, and a negative emotion is any emotion that is <u>not</u> owned and expressed. In other words, anger expressed is a positive emotion, and love <u>un</u>expressed is a negative emotion.

We could go a step further and redefine emotions and feelings. We could say that all expression is a "feeling" and all repression of expression is an "emotion." From this point of view, we want to strive to live our lives out of feeling rather than emotion.

With this explanation, it is easy to understand that depression is a repression of expression. In fact, much

38

of our emotional pain is just a repression of expression. Part of our enlightenment process, then, is to learn to express all feelings. Feelings are LIFE energy. Life is a feeling and feeling is life! Life is the natural feeling of the high self, and repression is the natural expression of the ego. The ego's fear keeps us from expressing our feelings.

Not any more! As you follow along in this book, you will little by little begin the process of releasing and shattering your old illusions. Way down inside of you, you have always known that something was wrong with the system. It didn't work, and now you are beginning to understand why.

When you begin to express from your true self, you will rekindle your zest and enthusiasm. You will reconnect with your inner spirit. Spirit is synonymous with enthusiasm. Spirituality is enthusiasm. It is a decision to live and not just survive. It is the decision to live and FEEL. It is saying "yes" to life. It is saying, "I EXIST! I CHOOSE LIFE! I AM!

CHAPTER NINE

Fear of Death

*It is difficult to live enthusiastically
when you are so afraid of dying.*

The next illusion we must deal with is that death is something to be afraid of. It is difficult to live enthusiastically when we are so afraid of dying. Why do we fear death so much? Do we fear that death will be the end of us and our identity, and that there is total nothingness after death?

By now, with all the literature available about near-death experiences and out-of-body experiences, we know beyond a shadow of a doubt that there is life after death. We also know it deep in our soul through our high self.

The real fear probably has to do with what we will experience after death - the heaven/hell theory. As a metaphysician, I believe and know that I create all things from the energy of my thoughts, attitudes, and expectations. I know that if I believe in a heaven, I will go to heaven, and if I believe in Hell, I will experience Hell. If I don't have any particular beliefs or if I don't believe in an afterlife, I will be in a sort of sleeping limbo.

Ultimately, I will go to the place that corresponds to my vibrations and my level of consciousness. According to universal law, we cannot stay in a place that doesn't match our vibrations. All things in the universe are energy vibrating at different rates. We are automatically magnetized to our corresponding vibrations. Like attracts like.

Perhaps we are associating death with pain. We are afraid of pain and torture. Again, we must survey the ways we cause ourselves pain and how we torture ourselves with our critical thoughts and self-judgments.

When we live out of the low self, we experience pain and death, but when we live out of our high self, we experience life and freedom from pain. When we live from the point of view of the high self, we attract safe and pain-free experiences, and we are loving to ourselves.

Many people are afraid of earth disasters and want to know where they can live safely. Take my advice and don't go to the "safe" places where all the fearful people are going, because all the fear will create an unsafe place. Just choose LIFE and you will be safe wherever you are. The only choice you will ever have to make is to exist or not - to live or not. If you choose life, you will continue to experience life, and you will be safe. The secret is to FEEL life and not just live it.

CHAPTER TEN

Death of the Ego

The only real death is the death of the ego.

The only real death that can ever happen is the death of the ego. It is the only part of us that can die. Unfortunately, when the ego dies the body also dies, because we have identified so strongly with the ego as a physical being. The two seem as though they are one.

Our <u>real</u> self (the deep self or high self), never gets to emerge. It stays hidden and untapped during our entire stay on earth. My teacher, Philip, has said that no human being has ever lived out of their deep self at this point in history (including Jesus, Buddha, Krishna, Mary, and other great spiritual figures). The identity with the physical body still remained. Even when the ego dies and the real self is left, there will be no "<u>body</u>" left because it died with the ego. We then have to come back for another round in the physical body, life after life after life. And still, we keep repeating the vicious circle.

What we must learn to do is drop the ego and let it die while we are still alive in a human body. The real self needs a persona with psychological constructs in order to operate as a real self. In the history of this earth, no one yet has reached their deep self, because the deep self is not individuated. It is all one essence and it is too threatening to the ego to give itself up.

We are in the process of learning to reach into our

deep self and let it emerge as we learn to stop identifying with the ego and thinking of ourselves as separate and detached from the whole.

The incessant yearning that we all seem to have never seems to be satisfied - no matter how much we eat, how much sex we have, or how much we meditate. What we really yearn to do is connect with the deep self, and unfortunately, the deep self is covered up with all the layers of the ego.

No matter how many lifetimes we live and no matter how spiritual we try to be, it will never work. Life will never be satisfying until the ego is dead and the real self emerges.

One way to achieve that is to start FEELING and stop thinking. We must connect with the <u>life</u> force within instead of the fear within. We must learn to be fully present in the moment instead of replaying the past or worrying about the future.

We must learn to breathe correctly by taking deeper breaths. The amount of breath you are willing to take <u>in</u> symbolizes the amount of life you are willing to experience, and the amount of breath you are willing to let <u>out</u> symbolizes the extent to which you are willing to surrender and turn your life over to the real self. Both breaths represent trust.

Dolphins teach us many things. Dolphins never need to sleep. (They breathe into, and out of, the heart. Both breaths go within to the heart. Dolphins operate out of the true self - the <u>real</u> self. Perhaps that is why we fail to understand their language. Their language is one of feeling and not thinking. Until we learn that language ourselves, we will never understand theirs.

43

CHAPTER ELEVEN

The Nature of God

There is nothing in the Universe judging you.
Only you judge yourself.

The next illusion that we must overcome is that there is a judgmental God. The concept of God has mostly been created in our image rather than the other way around. If we go back through history, we will see that when we were warlike, we created a warlike God. When we were critical and judgmental, we created a critical and judgmental God, and when we evolved into a more loving species, we created a more loving God.

We now have some evidence that our universe, and others, were created by more than one entity, and that perhaps there are overlords or gods for different areas of creation. These gods have different levels of proficiency and are evolving just as we are.

Michael Newton, a Canadian hypnotherapist, tells us in his book Journey of Souls, that his subjects speak of a God who purposely created a place where there is a lack of peace so we would strive harder. That God then expands as a result of what we learn.

Our Creator also expresses through us. If It didn't express, it would probably atrophy or shrink. We will probably never know all the answers to our questions about God, but I am quite certain that the purpose of life is to express, and I believe that Source is expressing through us in order to extend itself.

Since God and the Universe are composed of one

raw material (joy), it would make sense that God would not even be able to conceive of anger or judgment. An apple can only be an apple. Love can only be loving. Joy can only be joyful.

There is nothing in the universe judging you - only you yourself. Because you contain God particles of Spirit, your true self is God Spirit, and you are a Creator also. You create from your thoughts and beliefs, and what you experience is a result of those thoughts and beliefs.

There are no good or bad experiences - just experiences. There is nobody judging you - only you. If you like an experience, you can create more of it, and if you don't like an experience, you can change it. You judge it only because of the illusions you have been taught and have bought. When you begin to drop the illusions, you will begin to drop the judgments, and you will no longer create a judgmental God.

CHAPTER TWELVE

Your Total Self

*You are much bigger and vaster
than you ever realized.*

Having discussed God, it is now time to meet yourself - your <u>whole</u> self. Up until now, you have been aware of only a small fragment of yourself. You are much bigger and vaster than you ever imagined.

The next illusion to dispel is that you are a singular self. Not only do we have multiple personalities within us, we have personalities outside ourselves which up until now we have called "angels."

When part of Source particularized, the particles flew in different directions. Depending upon which direction they went, they became past lives, present lives, or future lives, but in reality they all happen at the same time. (When you are driving on the ground, you can't see the hills and valleys ahead because you haven't arrived there yet, but from an airplane above, you can look down and see them all at once.)

Some of those particles of ourselves are embodied and some of them are not embodied. Part of our brain keeps track of all those selves. (We actually have more than one brain, but I will save that discussion for my next book.)

All those selves are having experiences and are evolving little by little, just like the self in this lifetime. The particles we have in our present body are not the complete self. Eventually, all the parts of ourselves, inside and outside, must come together to create a "total" self.

We must gather all the parts of ourselves back together again, clearing and healing each part in the process. Upon becoming the Total Self, we then go back to Source, bringing more back than we started out with originally.

Some of our other selves direct and guide us along the way. These are our "angels" and guardian angels. We each have a "board of directors" guiding and directing <u>all</u> of our selves. They oversee the activities of the selves. They are the ones in charge, and they help us at all times (this is our "high self"). We needn't worry about understanding the big purpose, because it is unfolding perfectly with the guidance of our board of directors.

We are all doing this together. We will all be going home together, bringing our gifts of experience and feelings with us. We will go as a group just like the Mayans did and other cultures before that.

CHAPTER THIRTEEN

The Chakras

*The evolution of the soul
can be understood
through the chakra system.*

One of the ways we can understand our multiplicity, is to study the chakra system. Chakras are spinning vortexes of energy located in the physical body. The major chakras are located at the sites of the endocrine glands, and the minor chakras are located at various other sites in the body, such as the palms of the hands and the soles of the feet. We also have five major chakras outside the physical body, which are related to the holographic part of ourselves.

Each major chakra in the physical body represents an aspect of ourselves that is unique and separate. That self lives in its own universe with its own perspective and its own way of seeing things. The lower chakras could be thought of as the younger selves and the upper chakras could be thought of as the older selves.

The evolution of the soul can be traced and understood through the components of the chakra system. Each chakra is like one note on the scale. As you move higher, the vibration becomes faster, and the tone or pitch changes to a higher pitch. In addition, each pitch has a different color, and each pitch represents a different color of the rainbow.

Each chakra has a different function. Each of us is

meant to use all the colors of the rainbow as we create the palette of our life, but most people express themselves using only several colors of the rainbow. That is why so many people are bored and lifeless, and have trouble finding meaning in life.

If we take a closer look at each chakra, or spiritual center, we find the lowest major chakra located at the tailbone or root of the spinal column. According to Rosalyn Bruyere, the well-known healer and clairvoyant, this lowest center is related to our ability to just "be" and experience our "beingness". It is also related to how grounded we are, how connected we feel to the earth and earth life, and how well we feel our survival needs are being met. It is also related to our physical vitality and physical health. The personality of this first chakra is like a four-year-old because it is in the now, just "being", and it is the fun, vivacious part of ourselves.

The second chakra interacts with the world from a feeling perspective. Its only framework is feelings. Like a seven year old, this child lives life and reacts to life from the feeling center. It is mostly concerned with feeling safe, and that is why we call it the security center. This center is located in the lower belly, below the navel.

The third center or personality, is in the solar plexus area, and is the equivalent of 15-18 years of age. It is action and thinking oriented. It is our mental body, and it only "thinks." This is the personality within us that analyzes and figures things out.

These bottom three personalities are related to the external, material world and all its functions. We can already see that some people are feelers and live out of their second chakra, and others are thinkers and primarily use their third chakra. Still others are "be-ers" and prefer just to "hang out" and be in the moment in the first chakra.

The energy field around us contains a swirl of colors emitting from the chakras we favor. This energy field is called our "aura." Kirlian photography can actually photograph the colors around us which make us individual and unique and different from everyone around us. A well-grounded person who exercises a lot and has a strong earth connection, will have a lot of red in his aura. The feeler/creative type will have orange in the auric field, and the mental, reflective person will have the color yellow as a predominate color in her energy field.

Different countries and different cultures create certain distinct auras around people. Some cultures emphasize physical rituals, while others emphasize mental, intellectual, and scientific abilities. Still others value religion, meditation, and connection with the higher realms. No wonder it is difficult for different countries to understand each other and to relate to each other.

As we move into the heart center or green chakra, we move out of the self-oriented world of the low self, and into the realm of love and compassion for others. We can learn to become compassionate by the age of twenty, if our lower chakras are operating properly. The heart is the bridge between form and spirit, between earth and heaven. As we walk across this bridge, we cross over into the spiritual realms of higher spirit.

The first spiritual realm is at the throat area and is related to our ability to express our truth, whether it is through speaking, drawing, dancing, singing, or writing poetry. This is the personality that is able to express its true inner spirit, and it describes the way we respond from our spirit. The personality that resides in this area is like a wise sage. We all have a wise sage within. This level of vibration and expression is blue in color, therefore a person who is in touch with her inner spirit and is able to express that spirit, will have a lot of blue in her aura.

The inner visionary part of us lives in the forehead area and contains our intuitive and clairvoyant abilities. This being would ideally be in its forties, and is a vital part of us. If we don't have a vision or grand plan for our lives, then life will feel empty and meaningless. This part of us helps us follow our bliss, and guides us according to the higher meaning in our lives.

The seventh inner aspect of ourselves resides at the crown of the head and is connected to our Source in an attitude of trust and surrender. It is our ability to turn over our problems and worries to a Higher Power which, in turn, brings peace and serenity to our lives. Just remember that all seven parts are parts of your SELF. All seven inner personalities are your inner family. They are designed to work together and help each other. This is what is called integration of the personality. When you express your life from the points of view of these seven spiritual beings, you become the full color spectrum of the rainbow, and you _do_ find the pot of gold at the end of the rainbow.

Rainbow Chakra Exercise

1. Sit quietly and relax your body by taking some deep breaths. Release all tension and stress on the exhales.

2. Envision a bright red sun at your tailbone area. Let the sun begin to shine its rays of red energy throughout the whole area of the tailbone, and then let it spread throughout your whole body until you become a totally red person with a red aura. Let the rays return back to the tailbone area and stay there in a lovely ball of red energy. Let the ball of energy return to its normal and natural size, and then proceed to the next chakra.

3. Imagine a bright orange sun in the lower abdomen (4" below the belly button). Let the sun begin to shine its rays throughout the whole lower abdomen, and then let it spread throughout your whole body until you become a totally orange person with an orange aura. Let the rays return back to the lower abdomen and stay there in a lovely ball of orange energy. Let the ball of energy return to its normal and natural size, and then proceed to the next chakra.

4. Repeat the process using yellow for the solar plexus (stomach) area, green for the heart area, blue for the throat area, violet for the third eye area (above the nose, between the eyebrows), and white for the crown chakra (top of the head).

CHAPTER FOURTEEN

The Human Body

*The body has a consciousness of its own
and contains the clues to your future.*

One of the biggest illusions we have is that the body is less important than the spirit. Let's take a look at this human body that is made of flesh. After all, it was never a very comfortable place for the spirit to inhabit. As a spirit, we felt something like an astronaut walking around in a heavy space suit. Secondly, we started comparing our body to everybody else's body, and decided that we liked everybody else's better than our own. We wanted to trade ours in.

The only way to get another body is to lay this one down and come back and try on a new one. This is how we originally created "death." Even now, after trying many bodies, we are still not satisfied , and we tend to strongly reject our own physical body. We have learned to be more comfortable in them, but the exterior is never quite right: the hips are too big, the stomach is too bulgy, the hair is too gray or sparse, there are too many lines on the face, and so forth.

The truth is that the body is a crucial part of the big picture. It has a consciousness of its own and it contains the clues to our future in its DNA. In the next years to come, our bodies will begin to soften and the coded instructions in the DNA will allow us to become the real person we came here to be. Our life's purpose will be decoded and that purpose will proceed to unfold. As a result, there will be many changes in our personalities. What we used to hate, we might now love, and visa versa. Some people will go through dramatic personality changes as these DNA encodements open.

Our bodies are already undergoing some initiations with the energy changes and astrological influences. Some of the symptoms you might experience include dizziness, nausea, fatigue, aches and pains, headaches, forgetfulness, and many other symptoms.

In order to be as comfortable as possible in these coming times, just learn to relax and know that everything is in divine order and that this is one of the most exciting times in history. Get out of the fear of your low self, and open your being, without resistance, to the fabulous life energies pouring upon the planet. Only resistance, stress, and tension will cause you discomfort.

Trace minerals and amino acids are important at this time. You might want to soak in a bathtub of non-iodized sea salt water with trace minerals added. Gentle stretching exercises are also advised, along with sensible care of the body in general. Most of all, stay in a celebratory mood, because there will be much to celebrate.

CHAPTER FIFTEEN

Planet Earth

*One of our greatest illusions
is that heaven is greater than earth.*

Contrary to popular opinion, planet earth is one of the most beautiful and desirable places to be in the entire universe. There are spirit entities by the thousands waiting in line to come into this earthly experience. This planet is known as the "vacation" land. It is known to have many "flavors" of experience. We have hundreds of flavors here, whereas many other places may only have four or five.

Flavors are experiences of the senses and feelings. We have a spectacularly beautiful planet, with all sorts of beauty and textures to delight in. Somehow or other, many people have lost the thrill of being here. They think it is better somewhere else and they are sometimes anxious to go back home where "heaven" is.

It is a fallacy that heaven is somewhere out there in space and you can only experience it after you have left the body. First of all, you can't really go back home. You are different now. You have changed and have become more than you were before. If you were to go back to the place you came from, you would be bored to death. It would be too simple and repetitious for you, and you would soon long for something more interesting and varied.

Secondly, even if you went to the heaven of your

belief after you died, you would not be able to stay there long, unless your level of consciousness could consistently hold vast levels of joy and love.

The earth plane is a good place to practice. Heaven is <u>a state of consciousness</u>, and we can be in heaven right now during this earth life, if our state of consciousness matches heaven. I believe that there are different levels of heaven, according to how long and how much we can hold the state of joy.

There is much talk about "ascension" these days. Ascension is the ability to consistently hold life and joy in our mind, body, and spirit. This planet has become very dead, and most of the people here have become very joyless. The purpose of light workers everywhere is to restore life and joy to this planet.

Spirituality is simply going about your daily life with joy and exuberance and zest in your heart. It is the ability to feel intensely and passionately about something. It is feeling the vibrancy of LIFE flowing through your veins.

Most people are barely alive. They are surviving, but they have not connected with the pulse of life within their being. Stop for a moment and feel the life in your body. Intensify the energy so that you can feel it even more. If people would do this for even a few minutes every day, there would be less illness and disease. When you align yourself with life and choose to FEEL it, you give the signal to your inner being that you want to live and be healthy. Now is a good time to begin.

CHAPTER SIXTEEN

Finding the Answers

All answers are within you.
Stop looking outside yourself for them.

Another illusion is that answers are found outside of ourselves. We have been taught that God and heaven are outside of us, far away, and we must become perfect before we can reach either one of them. That idea was designed by the truth controllers so they could be in power. They sent us on long impossible trips to keep us occupied so we wouldn't claim our own power. In this way, they would be superior and we would be inferior.

It has worked so far, but we will no longer want to play that game. In the old days, the priests and fathers of the church had more power than kings because they had a so-called magical connection to God that no one else had. When others wanted to learn the secrets so that they could also be connected to God, the priests and churches had to invent a way to prevent competition. So they concocted stories and initiation processes to keep the people occupied for a long time so that they would not come into their own power.

The people were told that they had to meditate, chant, perform ablutions, give up earthly pleasures, experience deprivation and loneliness, and furthermore, it would take many years to learn to do it right.

This, of course, was a safe plan because the church leaders knew that most people wouldn't succeed because of the stringent requirements. It is said that the Ten Commandments came from a truth-controlling Overlord. All the "thou shalt nots" were a guarantee that the average person would feel great guilt and failure if they couldn't live up to the commandments. Guilt is very disempowering.*

We have created such devastating rules for ourselves that we can no longer be spontaneous and have fun. We are belabored with guilt and unworthiness. We have given up the beautiful pleasures of the earth because of these rules. No wonder we experience such mass depression and need to tranquilize away our feelings.

Are you beginning to feel some anger about this? I hope so, because it is your ticket back to life. Anger is vital, passionate, creative energy, and if you will just let yourself experience it and not judge it as bad, it will feel like vibrant life activated inside of you. Don't get stuck at the anger level; let the anger transmute into vital life and get on with the process of self-empowerment.

*Please understand that I am not opposed to Christianity. It has been a deep and important part of my life. I am simply against disempowerment in any form. I believe that the teachings of Jesus have been greatly misunderstood and misinterpreted, and that the church has withheld important information from us.

CHAPTER SEVENTEEN

Back to Feelings

We must learn to _feel_ more and _think_ less.

We have already learned the difference between emotions and feelings. Let's take a closer look at feelings so that we can begin to reclaim them.

First of all, they are much more important than people realize. We must learn to "feel" more and "think" less. Our Creator Source is not a THING, It is a FEELING. It is LIFE. It is JOY and LOVE. It is through the feelings of joy and love that we connect with Source, and not with the thoughts in our head.

On this planet, love is actually an emotion rather than a feeling. The basic emotions here on earth are guilt and love, and the basic feelings are joy and happiness. Guilt and love, the way we experience them, are repressed feeling. We repress feeling through guilt by feeling bad about the things we do, and we repress feeling through love because we have learned that love "hurts" and we are afraid of it.

If I asked you to open up and receive love, your body would probably close down, because it knows that love can hurt. But stranger yet, your body would probably resist joy because it is not used to feeling such a powerful energy.

I recall a time when I took a friend with me on a three day vacation. She was going through a divorce and was lonely without her family. Because of very limited funds, her family had never taken any trips or experienced the little pleasures of life. I took her with me to the North Shore of Minnesota. By the second day, as we were sitting by a creek with a little waterfall, she complained of feeling ill. We went back to our lodgings so that she could rest. When I asked her what caused her to feel sick, she said, "all the beauty was just too much for my system."

Joy can be like that. It can be too much for the body. We are not used to it. That is why we are not able to ascend at this time (leave the planet and take our body with us). We do not have enough joy to do it.

We must practice opening ourselves to more and more feeling - to more beauty, harmony, joy, tenderness, and gentleness. It is <u>feeling</u> that feeds us, and most people are starving.

The body needs light and energy to survive. Since we do not create enough energy food for ourselves, we have to stir some up by creating trauma and drama. The energy from the trauma and drama feeds us, but it is a vicious cycle because we have to keep creating more of it in order to survive.

The solution is to learn to <u>source</u> energy and feed our body with it. All we have to do is open our bodies by <u>feeling</u> safe, and then just go out into the universe and get a bunch of energy and feed ourselves from the bottom up.

Our body was created to accept and run energy up the spinal column and then feed and fill the body. The body, however, is afraid of the energies it doesn't understand, so it must feel absolutely safe before it is willing to open up. It is important not to label any energy "bad" because the body will close down and reject it. Energy is abstract. We have to format it so the body will know what it is before it will ingest it.

Once we learn to take the connotations off energy and teach the body that there is no such thing as bad energy, it will open up and feed itself more regularly. Remember, there is only one energy in the universe. It is only the labels we put on it that make it seem negative.

Since the body is afraid of love, most people don't really want love as much as they want <u>safety</u>. If you stop to think about it, the people you like to be around the most are the ones you feel safe with - not necessarily the ones who say they love you the most.

One of the ways we can heal ourselves is to stay in "feeling" (the language of the high self), and stay out of "emotion" (the language of the low self). It is <u>feeling</u> that heals us, not words. All the stories we tell our therapists are "ego" stories and nothing more. All the stories of woe and misery we tell are unimportant ego diversions. We must get back into feeling and stay away from emotion if we want to heal and restore ourselves.

In the long run, <u>spirituality is life</u> and we can <u>feel</u> life only if we face our fears, heal them, and release them. The bulk of our work is to get to know ourselves better, to become aware of our fears and angers, and to be willing to express more of our authentic self. That is what this book is about.

The real truth is that many of our spiritual leaders may appear calm and serene on the outside, but they have simply repressed their fear and anger because it is not "spiritual." They, too, have bought the system and are kept in line by the truth controllers. They may meditate and talk to God in a lovely way, but their personal and mental and emotional state may not be in very good shape because they must repress their own feelings in order to appear "good" and "kind" all the time.

This approach is <u>not</u> fun and spontaneous. It is false and misleading. I think we should let the gurus off the hook and let them be more authentic. We can do that when we stop looking outside ourselves for models of perfection. Now that we are dropping the illusions, we remember that we were all created in a state of perfection. All of us are equally perfect, and all of us are equally human.

CHAPTER EIGHTEEN

More on Feelings

*One of the lies you bought
is that you have to protect yourself
from negative energy.*

One of the most important things we must master is the way we use energy. As I have already said, all emotions are repressed feelings. We must work to free our energy so that feeling is flowing through us at all times.

In order to do that, we must remove the fear that accompanies our emotions. If we remove the fear, then the emotion will be transmuted into a "feeling." Since there is only one feeling - JOY, we would then be feeling good all the time.

Joy, of course, has many components. It is a combination of happiness, enthusiasm, inspiration, beauty, harmony, ecstasy, tenderness, and other "good feeling" energies.

Pain is just blocked joy, whether it is physical, mental, or emotional. We must learn how to unblock joy so that we can have health and happiness. It is not as hard as you think. It just takes a little practice and the willingness to change old habits.

You must first relax the body and release all tension. <u>All emotion is the result of tensing up the body.</u> Once you release the physical tension, you must help the body open and soften. The body will not open and soften unless it feels safe. It will feel safe after you teach it that all energy is the same and that only fear can cause pain because it causes the body to tighten up.

EXERCISE I: Taking the Label Off

1. Think about something you are angry about or have been angry about. Let yourself really feel the anger. In fact, intensify it and magnify it as much as you can.

2. Keep feeling it but take off the connotation that it is "bad."

3. Keep feeling it without the negative label. Begin to breathe your body open and relax all physical tension.

4. After achieving a relaxed open state, begin to notice how you are feeling. Just notice how the energy feels and describe it.

If you achieved a relaxed state, you will find that you experienced a vibrant energy filled with life and vital force. Once you took the negative connotation off anger and relaxed your body, you simply experienced the energy of vibrant life and happiness. It actually felt good! That good feeling is the only feeling you can have when no tension is present. It is the only energy in the universe.

EXERCISE II: Transmuting energy

Do the exercise again, but this time feel anxiety or worry or some other emotion that you would label negative. Feel the emotion but take the label off of it. Then relax and unblock the body so that the energy can flow through the body. (Remember to remind the body that it is entirely safe). Again, you will feel the <u>feeling</u> of life and joy.

This new insight and understanding will change your life, because your body will now be getting fed on a regular basis and will want more. It will now feel safe and will no longer waste energy trying to protect itself because it knows that only fear and tension can cause painful emotions. It will now stay open and slurp in the life energy that it has been craving, and it will cease to feel dead and starved to death.

EXERCISE III: Conscious Feeding

We can feed the body at any time or at any place using whatever energy is available. We can just imagine ourselves collecting a big chunk of energy or "junk" from the universe, condensing it into a block or ball of energy in front of us, and feeding ourselves with it from the bottom of our body to the top (taking it into the body at the tailbone area and letting it flow upwards throughout the body along the spine).

We can now see that all those rituals we performed to keep ourselves safe were unnecessary - just another way to scare ourselves and live out of the fear of the ego. It's a wonder we have any quality of life whatsoever with so much fear. Dropping illusions is the same as dispelling fear.

I often hear people say that they are afraid to go certain places or be around certain people because of the negative energy. The reason they feel negative energy is because they, themselves, are creating it in their own body as a result of tensing up and closing down from the fear or expectation of experiencing a negative energy.

If, instead, they would open up and expand and breathe freely, taking in all the energy around them, they would feel good and the body would feel fed rather than starved. Next time you are in a shopping mall or in a place with lots of people, just gather a big ball of it - junk and all - and feed yourself. It feels great!*

*The information contained in this chapter, including the exercises, is based on the channeled material of Sheradon Bryce. I strongly recommend her book, Joy Riding the Universe.

CHAPTER NINETEEN

NOW is the Best Place to Be

A true master is a master of energy.

A master is in a state of <u>feeling</u> all the time, and a master stays in the present moment where all the power is. <u>Now</u> is the moment of power.

If we want to be in a state of feeling joy and happiness all the time, we must learn to stay in the present moment. In order to do that, we must stay out of the ego because it is the nature of the ego to be worried or stressed about something most of the time. The ego is always in the past or future.

The ego has rules and regulations about everything, and it always has expectations based on its needs. It is those rules, regulations, and expectations (our belief systems) which keep us out of the present moment.

Being present in the moment is an attitude. It is an attitude of surrender or letting go. Since most people have great difficulty letting go, it is sometimes difficult to adopt this "surrender" attitude. To surrender means to be able to trust. It is not the nature of the ego (low self) to trust, and that is why we must begin to drop the ego.

Most people are so afraid of dying that they won't even let their fears die. They are also afraid of doing things alone, and they cling to the security of the group. It takes a courageous pioneer to ascend into the birth of their real Self, but a few brave souls have managed to do it and are helping us learn to do it too. Those few souls have made a bridge for the rest of us to follow. An individual birth ascension is an ascension in consciousness only. It is not a "popping off" the planet. However, as more and more individuals experience their individual births, they will start coming together in small groups to eventually experience a group ascension (probably around the year 2,012).

According to our scientists, there is a gigantic death process happening in our universe right now. About 80% of our universe has already died, and the rest is in the process. It is just a natural part of the life/death/life cycle. As we leave here, we are birthed somewhere else.

The birth process is not always comfortable, just as it is not comfortable for a baby to sustain the birth contractions of the mother. It can feel as though you are being squished to death and can't breathe, and the anticipation of the next contraction can cause fear.

If we could stay in a relaxed state, breathing as naturally and normally as possible, floating in the present moment and totally letting go and trusting the process, we would experience very little pain or difficulty. It is the anticipation that makes us tense, and it is the tension that causes the pain.

As you can see, the ability to let go and relax and focus on the present moment will become more and more important as we experience the challenges of the coming times.

Since loving ourselves can only happen in the present moment, and since loving ourselves has nothing to do with what we do but rather what we are, we must be willing to stop being so concerned with what we do and start allowing ourselves to simply be and be happy with our beingness, whoever we are.

Our worth or state of beingness has never been an

68

issue. Our worth is perfect and has always been perfect. Only the false issues of the ego and the focus of attention away from the moment have led us astray.

Perhaps the original purpose of meditation was to get us to relax, let go, and settle into the moment, but it lost much of its effectiveness when we began to focus outward to the realms far away and abandoned our own wisdom and knowingness.

The word "mindfulness" might describe a more helpful approach. It teaches us to be more aware of what is going on around us right now and helps us to appreciate it and resonate with it as we stay fully aware and fully present in our body. Mindfulness is connected to the vibration of life, and we become more <u>conscious</u> as a result.

The best meditation is to sit and feel the life in your body, claiming life, and connecting with it. The birthing process is one of "coming to life." It is not a dying process where we leave the body and "trance out."

MEDITATION

To meditate means to increase your clarity and become more conscious. It means that you are fully present with all of your power. If you are like everybody else, you give your power away all day long. Every time you <u>react</u> to the external world, you give away your power.

The only real power we have is the power within. Our external power is of illusion, because it is based on the false power of the ego and low self. In order to have power as a creator, we must fuel our <u>inner</u> power system.

The inner power system gets depleted every time we have thoughts about the past or the future. Most people send their energy to the past and continually recreate past wounds, or they are projecting worries into the future. One way or the other, they have very little energy or time for the present.

We must become more and more aware of what we do with our power (our spirit - our high self). If our thoughts are not in the present, then we are sending our spirit off to the past or future. We can learn from meditation what thoughts and perceptions own us and steal our power away from us.

Meditation Exercise For Energy Awareness

1. Sit in a room with a mirror. The light should be very low so that you can barely see yourself. You should see a hazy impression of yourself.

2. Just sit and look at yourself. Describe the person you see in the mirror. Look beyond the physical appearance, and describe the essence of this person. What is your deepest impression of this person?

3. After you have looked at yourself in the mirror like this for awhile, your mind will probably begin to wander. Notice where your mind goes. Notice what thoughts you begin to think. These are the thoughts and perceptions that own you and steal your power. Any thought that takes you away from the present controls you. Learn to keep your focus of attention on the present.

CHAPTER TWENTY

Entrainment Release

We can learn to create any feeling we want.

The next step is to begin to release all the "creases" of tension deep within the body. Philip, the non-physical teaching entity who speaks through Sheradon Bryce in Arizona, calls these creases "entrainments." He teaches us that entrainments are those little irritants and worry vibrations that are buried deep within us. They are vibrations that come from mass consciousness and keep us restricted and imprisoned. Philip teaches us how to release them quickly.

Releasing Entrainments

1. Relax your body and breathe deeply for a few minutes, letting go of the tension and stress in your body.

2. Go deep within and find a place where you sense a slight state of worry. Allow yourself to intensify and magnify it, and then condense it into a little strip or band and cut it or snip it with an imaginary pair of scissors or whatever seems appropriate for you. (I use a laser sword of light or I pinch it with my fingers, whatever it takes to release it. If the entrainment is hard like a tree branch, I use a power saw.)

3. Feel the subtle shift within your body as it releases, like a rubber band cut in two.

4. Now focus upon another entrainment vibration (they usually come in little groups), amplify it, coagulate it, and cut it.

5. Keep repeating the process.

6. Now feel the pulse of life in your being - the joy within - and let yourself really feel it. You will be able to sustain this joy for longer and longer periods of time as you learn to release entrainments.

7. Even as you feel the life and joy in your being, you will feel subtle entrainments beneath the joy. Amplify and focus them to make them stronger and more tangible, then cut or snip them and feel the subtle shift within you as you feel freer and softer.*

Entrainment release will be an important and helpful technique to use during these times of stress and tension as we experience the powerful energies and vibrations of the birth we are experiencing. We can learn to increase our cellular vibration or decrease it as we wish. In this way, we can create any feeling we want. That is how we become a master of our feelings and a master of our destiny.

CHAPTER TWENTY-ONE

The Coming Years

*For those of you
who have been living other people's truths,
it is time to reclaim yourself
and live out of your own integrity.*

As we move into the new millennium, we are going to experience some fascinating and challenging things. We will be making a shift in consciousness, and we will very literally be creating our own reality.

If you have been acting out of your own integrity and your own truth, you will be comfortable with the shift. For those of you who have been living other people's truths, it is now time to reclaim yourself and be true to yourself.

As a quickening comes, you will want to relax and have fun and enjoy yourself as much as possible. There is much to celebrate and there is much to experience. If you can stay light-hearted, you will probably enjoy every moment of this gigantic shift.

You will be coming into your own power and will be doing what you came to do. After the DNA breaks open and modifies the personality, you will experience new zest and vitality and passion for life.

Since we are all doing it together, we are experiencing a major shift in consciousness. As the intensity is released, there will be many people are not able to handle the intensity, and the result is increased crime and violence. We each need an outlet through which we can express the intensity of the incoming frequencies, whether it is through our work, politics, religion, or personal life.

You will have the choice of expressing your intensities through fear or through excitement and enthusiasm. You will walk your talk and it will be the walk of fear or the walk of life.

We will experience the birth of two basic personalities. One will be birthed here in linear time, and one will be birthed outside of this reality. As a result, we will be able to experience which reality we choose, and we will never be trapped in only one reality again.

Just sit back, relax, and enjoy the process. We will experience many shifts and adjustments as we move through the turn of the century. The main survival tools that you will need are to remember to be yourself and stay in your own integrity, to stay in a feeling of fun and joy, and to stay out of fear, judgment, and guilt. Above all, don't externalize God. BE God. Remember, you are a Creator. You can't know God, you can only BE God.

CHAPTER TWENTY-TWO

A Time For Healing

The relationship you have with your inner child
is the most important relationship you have.

Entrainment release and learning how to stay in feeling rather than emotion will be the best tools for healing as we deal with the energy intensities of this time.

The old systems don't work anymore. We can no longer solve our problems using the old systems. For example, in the past we would rehash our personal history with a therapist and relive our old pain. From my point of view as a practicing counselor, all those stories of our past are just "ego" stories and reliving them each time we tell them is just keeping us in our low self. All the talk about our past does us no good unless the therapist teaches us how to access the high self and change the radio station from P-A-I-N to G-A-I-N.

All we have to do is remember to listen to our inner conversation and change the channel if we don't like what we are hearing. Our inner "child" and our inner "parent" are often at odds, and it would help us immensely if we learned to identify these inner voices of our inner parent and inner child.

Whatever happened in our childhood is not relevant to our present healing process. What is relevant is what is going on with the inner child today. Our parents of the past are not responsible for the problems of today.

Our parents of the past cannot help our inner child of today. Our inner child lies within us and we, as it's parent, are responsible for this child. It is our <u>own</u> parenting skills which are important.

As a loving parent, we must listen to the needs of our inner child, and we must also be aware of our needs as an adult parent. We must be able to solve the conflicts of the inner child and parent by finding a solution that meets the needs of both. In other words, we will want to find a win/win solution.

There are several ways you can work with this system. One way is to take a piece of paper and a pencil and in the left column write a question to your inner child and in the right column write the answer.

EXERCISE: Connecting With Your Inner Child

1. Sit calmly, relax, and take a few deep breaths.

2. Think of a question that you would like to ask your inner child like "How are you today?" Ask this out loud and then write the question in the left hand column on your sheet of paper.

3. Let your mind connect deep within you, and feel or sense a response from your inner child. Don't try to think of an answer with your conscious mind. Let the answer come to you. Write down the <u>first</u> thing that comes to you.

4. Write the response exactly as it comes to you in the right column of your sheet of paper.

5. Continue the dialogue by asking questions like, "Dear inner child, what do you need most from me today?" or, "What would you most like to tell me?" Listen to the responses without judgment or criticism, and then thank your child for talking with you.

You will be surprised at some of the answers you receive from your inner child. The inner child is honest and truthful and will tell you what it needs in a very frank manner. It is important to listen to these needs and then find some way to meet them. The most important thing for you to remember is to listen without judging or criticizing. We tend to parent the way we were parented.

This relationship with our inner child is the most important relationship we have, because that child is with us our whole lifetime. It is the state of our inner child that determines the quality of our everyday life.

When your inner child begins to feel safe and loved, you will experience life very differently. You will no longer have that knot in your stomach or the constant feeling of worry and anxiety.

The inner child is the <u>feeling</u> part of us, and the inner parent is the <u>thinking</u> part of us. If we are feeling lonely, rejected, and sad, that is the inner child part of us, and if we are thinking and analyzing or trying to figure things out, that is our inner parent.

The inner parent may have a deadline at work while the inner child wants to play and have fun. This is an inner conflict, and it is up to you as a loving parent to find a way to meet the needs of both selves. You might decide to finish your work and then stop at the park and eat an ice cream cone on the way home. This would be an example of a win/win situation. It is important for you to keep your promises so your inner child will learn to trust you.

A second way to work with your inner child has been developed by Lucia Capacchione. It involves using your non-dominant hand as you write the answers from your inner child, and your dominant hand when the inner parent speaks. The inner child might want to draw a picture of itself for you. This method has been successful for many.

Whatever method you choose, this is important work. Since mastery is self-awareness at the deepest level, this is one of the best ways to become self-aware.

CHAPTER TWENTY-THREE

Guilt and Shame

Shame is the feeling
that something is <u>wrong with us</u>,
and guilt is the feeling that we have <u>done</u> something
wrong.

One of the by-products of inner child work is the discovery of inner shame and guilt. Shame and guilt stifle life more than anything else. Shame is the feeling that something is wrong with our being, and as a result we fear abandonment. Guilt is the feeling that we have done something wrong and we fear punishment.

The truth of the matter is that we run on the energy of guilt and shame just like a car runs on the energy of gasoline and oil. The problem is that guilt and shame are pollutants just like gasoline and oil. Most people take better care of their cars than they do of their own internal emotional system.

Most of our emotional symptoms are based on shame or guilt. Instead of treating depression and masking the symptoms, it would be a good idea to look at the shame/guilt factors.

Let's take a look at guilt first. There is practically nothing in our lives which does not produce guilt. We feel guilty for sleeping too late, for eating too much, for not working hard enough, for being late for an appointment, for not telling the truth, for not calling our mother, etc.. We even feel guilty when others feel bad!

Unfortunately, guilt is lack. It is lack of life. It is a deadness in the center of our being. We basically have one choice. Do we choose life or do we choose guilt? Remember, there is only one <u>emotion</u>: guilt, and there is only one <u>feeling:</u> life. Emotion is always a repressed feeling.

If we choose life, then we must learn to express ourselves without guilt. Expression is life! We have become such conformists that we have lost any sense of who we are. We are so concerned about being accepted, and we are so caught up in the role of trying to be nice and "good," that we have lost much of our honest, spontaneous life expression.

The number one thing that frightens us most is expressing ourselves or being expressed upon. The most important thing we can ever accomplish, is to learn to express without guilt.

Guilt, in a way, keeps us safe. It keeps us from doing the things that might make us look bad to others. It helps us stay in our proper place and therefore feel safe. That is the way of the low self. It is the choice of fear and not life.

Since a master is always working on self-awareness, you will now be given a chance to find out how much guilt you have, or how much you lack spontaneous life expression.

EXERCISE: Expressing Yourself Freely

Part A

1. Close your eyes and imagine yourself all alone on a stage. There is no one else in the universe.

2. Allow yourself to get in touch with the true feelings deep inside you that represent your own truth from your own authentic self. <u>Feel</u> it emotionally.

3. Begin to express anything and everything you feel truthfully.

4. After a few minutes, observe how you might be limiting yourself, and notice if you were judging yourself in any way.

Part B

1. Close your eyes and imagine that you are on a stage in front of a large audience.

2. Allow yourself to get in touch with your true feelings about something that has been bothering you. You are very angry.

3. Speak out loud and enact it. Act it out as you <u>feel</u> it.

4. Stop to observe your level of guilt.

These exercises will help you be more aware of the level of guilt in your everyday life so that you can be aware of how you close down the feeling of life every time you feel guilty.

We often feel guilty when we get angry. Anger without guilt is the expression of life! The most important thing we can ever learn to do is express ourselves without guilt. We can learn to do this when we drop the illusion that there is something judging us.

I have already stated that there is no punishing God in the universe. It is our own low self that judges and criticizes. As long as we stay in the low self, we will always be in guilt and we will rarely feel life and vitality. A master is the person who chooses to align with the high self and a higher perspective.

The higher perspective remembers that we are spirits who have chosen to take on a physical body so that we can experience the joys of life on the earth plane. We didn't come here to suffer. We came here to learn how to overcome our fears so that we could experience joy, happiness, and the wonderment of one of the most beautiful planets in the universe.

We came here to expand our consciousness, heal our limitations, and change our old negative patterns. We came here to learn to express our true being in all situations in a human body. We came here to experience LIFE, and life can only be experienced when we express without guilt.

Because we have been criticized and judged over and over in our formative years, most people walk around with a deep sense of shame. Shame is so deep and insidious that most people are not even aware of it.

We are experiencing shame when we withdraw from people and feel like we don't belong. Shame is when we try to be perfect so we won't be judged. Shame is when we hide our feelings with an arrogant exterior so that we can fend people off before they attack. Shame is when we deny we have problems or when we become enraged at little things in order to hide our sense of inadequacy.

Anytime we hear the message, "You are not good enough, you don't belong, you are not a nice person, you are not lovable," we will experience shame.

We can befriend our shame or we can treat it with hatred. We can realize that all of us have it. It is a normal part of life, and we can learn to accept it, make peace with it, and respect it as a teacher.

EXERCISE: Making Peace With Your Shame

1. Sit for a few minutes and reflect upon the ways you have experienced "shaming" from your parents, church, friends, teachers, or work place.

2. Reflect on the ways you have dealt with shame through denial, withdrawal, rage, exhibitionism, perfectionism, depression, etc...

3. Speak to your shame using the voice of your higher self as you remind yourself that you are okay just the way you are, that shame is a fact of life, and it is normal to have defenses.

4. Resolve to affirm and accept yourself instead of looking for approval from others.

5. Remember that all beings are inherently worthy as sons and daughters of Creator/Source. No amount of criticism or judgment can reduce your worth. You, yourself, cannot be of less worth than anybody else. You can only <u>perceive</u> yourself to be of less worth. Begin to change your perceptions and you will begin to change your world.

CHAPTER TWENTY-FOUR

Processing Your Feelings: Healing Your Life

Are you a creator or a victim?
The answer to that question
determines your whole life.

Everything that we have ever experienced, we have created according to our perceptions. We can't be feeling what we are feeling unless we are "thinking" it. First we have to <u>think</u> and then we <u>feel</u>, so whatever we are feeling is a result of our thinking. If we are <u>feeling</u> fear, then we are having a fearful thought.

If we have a certain feeling, it is because we perceive something in a certain way. It is our perceptions, and never the circumstances, that are the problem. We observe something, and then we perceive it according to our beliefs.

If we perceive something from our low self, we will experience fear, anxiety, worry, and concern. All of our "negative" feelings are a result of our insecurity, and all insecurity comes from the low self. We can never experience anything but insecurity until we raise the frequency of our perception from the lower part of our body (the low self) to a higher part of the body (the high self). The high self dwells in the kingdom of the heart and above.

EXERCISE I: Relocating Your Fears

Think of a fear or insecurity that you have and notice where it is located in the body. Then just raise it to a higher chakra or location in the body.

EXERCISE II: Changing Your Feelings

Imagine that your aura is like a huge bubble that extends around you fifty feet out from your body. Breathe in and pull the bubble closer to you so that it is now only 30 feet from your body. Exhale, then breathe in another time, this time pulling your auric bubble much closer to you (about 10 feet from you). Exhale, and once again as you breathe in, pull your aura very close to you (about six inches).

Your aura is now like a cocoon around you. You will be able to feel the presence of yourself quite clearly. Now <u>feel</u> the presence of love in your heart area. Let that love energy shine out like the rays of the sun, filling your cocoon until you quite literally experience the feeling of love throughout your whole being. You have now changed fear and insecurity to an entirely new feeling, and you did it all by yourself as a creator choosing how you want to feel.

We are winners when we think and perceive from our high self. This is called "channeling" our high self in our everyday life. Thoughts and feelings are just energies. We can change energies. We can transform them; we can transmute them into any feeling we want.

Everything depends upon our intent. If it is our intent to heal, then we will learn to be consciously aware of the things which need to be healed. If it is our intent to punish ourselves by thinking the same negative thoughts over and over, then that is another choice.

If it is our intent to grow, learn, and evolve, then we will learn to become aware of our experiences and emotions, treat them with compassion, change the frequency by changing our thoughts and perceptions, and as a result, become masters of our experiences.

YOU ARE NOT YOUR EMOTIONS

You must always remember that you are not your emotions. You are a person having an experience. If you are currently experiencing hopelessness, it is not the same as you - you are not hopelessness; you are a person <u>experiencing</u> hopelessness because of the thoughts you are thinking. Ask yourself, "what would I have to be thinking in order to create a feeling of hopelessness?"

If it is your intent to feel good, then you will want to make it a point to routinely be aware of your thoughts so that you can change them if they are creating a negative feeling.

It is important to note that you will be most miserable when your thoughts are in the past or the future. You will always feel best when you are focused in the present.

The first step in working with your emotions is to realize that emotions, including negative ones, are a natural part of being human. You will want to learn to accept and affirm anything that you are thinking and feeling, and not reject it.

If you are feeling sad, then you, a person of worth and beauty, are experiencing sadness. The sadness is separate from you. You couldn't be observing it unless it was separate from you. Just accept your experience by acknowledging and affirming it. This emotion of sadness is a real living child of energy within you. Treat it with love and tenderness as any loving parent would do.

ARE YOU A CREATOR OR A VICTIM?

We are all either creators or victims. If we believe that we have no choices and that we are powerless in life, we will live life from a victim point of view. If we take responsibility for our lives and are aware of how we create our experiences from our beliefs and perceptions, we will live life from the point of view of a creator. If we create something we don't like, then we can create something else that we like better.

The most important decision we will ever make is whether we are a victim or a creator. According to universal law, it can't be both ways. Either we are all creators or we are all victims. If we are all creators (which we are), then everybody is creating their life perfectly for their growing and evolving needs. They do not need us to judge them, help them, or rescue them. From the higher picture, they are creating every scenario in their life perfectly. If there are only creators, there can be no victims. We must not ever think of another person as a victim..

Some people might think that Christopher Reeve is a victim of a terrible accident which he had nothing to

88

do with. Others of us believe that he planned the whole event before he came into this lifetime so that he could be an inspiration to others on a world level. In this way, he is able to be a living model of how to overcome adversity; he is a perfect example of how the mind can transcend the limitation of the body. By having his accident and capturing the attention of the world, he can be a teacher to the masses and we can all have a living example of how to overcome limitation.

From a higher level, everyone is setting up circumstances in their life in a purposeful way. The mean neighbor next door is creating his experiences perfectly in order to grow or learn in some way. His meek wife is also a creator and has chosen the relationship in order to learn valuable lessons which will serve her well on her soul journey throughout time.

You must decide whether you are a creator or a victim and understand yourself accordingly. If you are a creator, then you have created <u>everything</u> for a reason and you have created it perfectly <u>without exception</u>, even though your low self doesn't understand that. If you don't like something, you have the ability to change it.

If you believe yourself to be a victim, then you are focused on the external world of the low self, and you are living a life of illusion, limitation, and untruth.

If you know that you are a creator, you will go within to your real place of power and create from an inner world of wisdom and higher intelligence. The only choice we ever have in the moment is where we choose to place our focus of attention - on the outside world of the low self (the victim) or on the inside world of the high self (the creator).

89

CHAPTER TWENTY-FIVE

Redefining God

The world is now insane.
Almost the entire population of the planet
lives life from the low self.

The above quote may seem extreme, but if you remember that the main ingredients of the low self are fear and guilt, you will soon see that most humans are stuck in an endless cycle of fear and worry, judgment and criticism, and guilt, guilt, and guilt. It is indeed time for a new birth.

If we are ever going to be free of our fear and guilt, we will have to work backwards and redefine the areas where our patterns are stuck the most.

Philip has taught me the true story of creation and our purpose in life, and although it was difficult for me to accept at first, I now understand and embrace the entire concept. I went through a deep and long grieving process as I let go of my past beliefs, but little by little I began to experience a new strength and freedom.

At the time I was first exposed to Philip's teachings (the channelings of Sheradon Bryce), I was a Christian mystic with a close and personal bond with Jesus. Jesus once appeared to me in my meditation room, and when I asked him why he had come, he said, "because you asked." I realized then that we really do get what we ask for.

According to Philip, the archetype of Christianity has focused almost exclusively on the pain, suffering, and poverty of Christ, and as creators we then experience pain, suffering, and poverty if we try to be Christ-like. The more we try to live like Jesus, the more we will experience suffering and betrayal, because this is the way universal law works. We become the archetype and live all the parts of it.

Philip says that we are midwives for the new birth, and in order to have a <u>live</u> birth, we must bring life to the planet in the form of joy and happiness. Philip says that we don't have a single archetype on earth that gives us permission to experience joy and magic. As a result, there is very little life on the planet.

Since this is the most important time in all of history as we rapidly move into the time of the birth, it is crucial that we focus on <u>feeling</u> life and vital force. If we are feeling guilty for not being spiritual enough, then we are not doing the job we came to do as a midwife trying to deliver a live, healthy baby.

Through our own human low selves, we have turned Christianity and other religions into depressing episodes of martyrdom and suffering with rules and regulations we could never follow. As a result, we walk around like zombies filled with guilt and low self-worth.

It is crucial that we begin to develop new gestalts as creators, so that we can move out of the old lethargy into a new time of magic and fulfillment. We have many master entities coming to earth to show us the way back to freedom and true spirit. They have come to remind us to stop looking for God externally and to look within to our own magnificence.

The controllers of truth, and even our own ego, would like to keep us imprisoned forever in our old prejudices and misconceptions, but it is time to move out of the darkness into the light of the universal sun, which is imprinting us with the new blueprint of the future and a new energy of life and passion.

CHAPTER TWENTY-SIX

The Refining Years

*Your brain must let go of this reality
in order for you to be born
into a new reality.*

There are many ways we keep ourselves chained to the old low self reality. Only the low self sees others as victims for us to fix, rescue, help, or save. One of the ways we disempower others and give away our own energy is to believe that someone else needs help. We focus so much on others that we literally glue ourselves into earth reality, making birth to another place impossible.

One of my greatest teachers, Sabe Loco, is a new entity channeled by Sheradon Bryce in Tucson, Arizona. Sabe has come to show us the way into a new universe. He tells us that "voyeuring" other people's lives in order to rescue and save them is a "perversion," just like peeking into another person's private space is a perversion. This keeps us attached to the illusion.

He says that the universe operates on one respectful principle: "Let nature take care of nature." In other words, stay out of other people's lives and focus on your own. If your energy is going out to others, you will not be centered in your own life energy and you will not have enough life to experience the ascension that accompanies the birth.

In the world of metaphysics and spirituality, many

people are so busy healing others that they forget to work on their own issues. Even well-intended healers and counselors don't always understand the true effects of energy on others.

For example, it is a popular practice for healers to perform absent healings. Could it be possible that absent healing can interfere with a person's natural healing process, simply because we don't know what the higher picture is for the other person? How can we possibly assume to know what another person needs?

As creators, we must honor each other's creations. If another creator chooses illness for a lesson, we should not automatically interfere. We must also understand the concept of amplification. When we send energy to something, it amplifies it. If we send energy to someone in pain, we are making it more intense and quite possibly adding to the pain. When we send energy to a cancer cell, could it be that we are actually giving more life to it by our focus upon it? Energy flows where attention goes.

We are now learning that the less we focus on an illness the faster the recovery. If we define an illness using a specific word like "cancer," we have given the person a label of energy to wear. Every single person who participates in this labeling process will add their energy to that belief and pretty soon we will have to heal 20 people in order to heal the one who has cancer.

The only <u>true</u> healing in the eyes of the universe, according to Sabe Loco, is when you hold someone in the attitude of perfection <u>with</u> their cancer or illness. If you can only see them as perfect without the cancer, or if you purposely try to see them or envision them without the cancer, you may be interfering in the natural

94

process of nature and the universe.

Suppose a woman comes to you because she has been unable to have a baby. As a knowledgeable healer, you know what to do, and you help readjust her vibrations so that she can have a baby. You may feel good that you have helped her, but you may have now made it more difficult for her to go through the universal birth process that is about to happen.

It will be more and more difficult for women to have babies during this time in history, because in order to get pregnant, the mother's body must vibrate at exactly the rate of the earth itself. As the frequencies of our bodies begin to vibrate faster and faster in preparation for the universal birth, it will be harder and harder to get pregnant. As you can see, we can't always know the bigger picture, so perhaps it is best not to interfere even at the rudimentary level.

If we can stay objective and not get emotionally involved and pulled into the problem, we will be centered in our own energy and that will be more supportive and helpful than anything we could do or say.

We must also watch our prayers for others, because prayers are energy, too. Are you sending a prayer because you perceive the person to be a victim? If they are a creator (and everybody is), then they are creating perfectly what they need to learn, and we could learn to honor their creations and not interfere. If we perceive them to be a victim, then we are playing god in order to rescue and save them. Anytime we think we have to help someone else, we are saying that they are not doing it right and we have a better answer. Isn't that being a bit arrogant?

Instead of sending our energy horizontally to others, we could send our prayers vertically to our high self and ask our high self to do the appropriate thing for the person's highest good. Even that is not necessary, because the person's high self is already working at a higher level.

For every pain we try to heal, I believe that we can take on that pain somewhere in our own energy field. Healers and helpers are notorious for taking on the energies of others and are very often burned out or ill themselves. From Sabe's point of view, there is <u>no</u> time when interference is warranted for any reason. Many people help others only to feel better about themselves. It gives them ego satisfaction and helps them feel worthwhile and worthy, but it is a cover up for low self-esteem and the fact that they don't have a life of their own. They are simply using others to feel good about themselves.

I am truly beginning to understand that if we stick to creating our own life and honoring each other as a creator, we will be more in accordance with universal law. We can learn to trust other people to take care of themselves. <u>Let nature take care of nature.</u>

Am I saying that we should never help others, especially when they ask us to? No, I am saying that in order to help others, we must not have the attitude of fixing them, changing them, rescuing them, or even trying to help them. We can most help them by staying in our own energy and observing them objectively without getting emotionally involved. We can then tell them what we observe, and they can learn from our honest, objective answers. They will feel honored and supported, and they will receive what is most helpful for them according to the big picture. In order to be helpful, we must not become emotionally involved. We must simply mirror to them what we see and observe objectively.

For those of you who truly enjoy and love hands-on healing work, I recommend that you go into a playful state of joy, and when you are completely filled with that joyful playfulness and one with it, place your hands on the body you wish to heal. This, in my estimation, is the highest form of healing energy work. Have fun, and channel that energy. You will love it, and so will the recipient!

CHAPTER TWENTY-SEVEN

Ten Powerful Suggestions For Enlightenment

The most powerful techniques are the most simple.

I like things that are simple and easy. I have found that the most powerful techniques are the most simple. For this chapter, I would like to focus on ten guidelines that could be called "the ten commandments for happy living." I think happy living and enlightenment are the same thing.

I can see how these ten commandments make up the ten chain links of my life. By observing my day to day life, I can see which ones are strong and I can see which ones are weak. I think it is good for all of us to identify our weakest link and begin to strengthen it. These 10 commandments also help me wake up and remember who I am.

1. <u>Stay in the Now</u>. This commandment is the hardest one for me. Because of the nature of my work, I am always working ahead to plan classes and events. When I studied shamanism in Hawaii I learned that all power comes from being connected with the present moment. It is crucial to stop dwelling in the past and stop worrying about the future if we want to become fully engaged in the moment. It is in the light of the moment that enlightenment comes.

When we are in a state of constant worry or anxiety, the light diminishes. The future is created from what we are doing and thinking <u>now.</u> Our life is like the software of a computer. What we put <u>in</u> comes <u>out</u>. We create our future from the software we put in, and the results are exactly what we put in. If I spend ten minutes today feeling happy, two hours feeling anxious and worried, thirty minutes feeling resentful, four hours feeling fear and doubt, and seventeen hours feeling guilty, that is exactly what I will spit out for tomorrow's menu. We create our reality much more exactly than we ever realized. Almost all of the negative emotions we experience come from rehashing the past or worrying about the future. If we could stay centered in the present moment, we would be creating a very different life.

2. <u>Let Go.</u> Another thing that keeps us in worry is our lack of trust in ourselves and the universe. This universe is totally supportive of us, but we have to <u>let</u> it support us.

When I was a youngster learning to swim, I was like a fish, and I loved to dive deep under the water and explore the bottom of the lake. I could do all the strokes effortlessly, but I could not learn to float. In order to float, I had to "let go" totally and I just couldn't trust that the water would hold me up. The strange thing is that when we do let go <u>all the way</u>, we are supported completely. The amount of abundance and love we have in our lives is directly related to our ability to let go and <u>receive</u> from the universe.

We must learn to take vacations and breaks from our fears and our need to control everything in order to feel safe. That is the job of the high self, and once we turn over all our worries and concerns to the high self, we will see how well it works. The low self doesn't deal well with life's problems. We must turn them over to the high self and then get out of the way and trust the results. It really works!

LETTING GO WITH YOUR BREATH

Exercise 1: Breathing is a good way to learn to let go. Every time you exhale, let go of the tension in your body, and let go of your worries and concerns. Breathe in the peace and safety of the moment and just let go.

Exercise 2: Breathe deeply, dropping all tension, and relax, letting your mind drift within. Imagine a beautiful setting that makes you feel good. Just sit in this setting and begin to think about all of your concerns - your bills, your health, your work, your relationships. Let the feeling build up until you feel burdened and overwhelmed. Just as you are feeling the most overwhelmed, imagine that a bright and beautiful light-- symbolizing your high self-- appears in front of you. This light says to you, "Give me your burdens. Give me your concerns. Give me your problems. I am here to take them from you. That is my function, and that is what gives me the most pleasure and happiness. Give me all of your worries and place them in my light."
See yourself taking all your sacks and suitcases of stuff and putting them in the light. See them dissolve in the light and disappear into the light. Feel the relief, and feel how much lighter you feel. Resolve not to take back the problems, Feel trust, and just let go.

3. Feel, don't think. The third commandment for happy living is to FEEL, not think. Feel the moment.

100

Feel the life within you. Feel the life around you. This commandment reminds us to FEEL LIFE and stop thinking so much. Feeling is energy with knowledge, and thinking is knowledge without energy.

4. <u>Stay in Your Own Integrity</u>. Live your life from your own truth. Honor your own ethics and principles, and stay true to your own inner spirit. Tell the truth and live your truth.

5. <u>Have Fun.</u> When we learn to trust ourselves, we begin to have fun. Most of us are much too serious, especially those of us in the field of spirituality. When I asked Philip what I needed most to work on, he said, "lighten up and don't be so serious. Be weird, be spontaneous, and be creative. Do things in a new and spontaneous way. Be atrocious and comical and fun-loving. Express yourself in as many ways as possible and don't worry about what other people think. If they think you are weird, then you know you are on the right track. If other people want to close down and be dead, let them."

Above all, don't get stuck in victimhood. Victims don't have any fun. Victimhood weakens you and keeps you from healing, and what is more fun than healing!

6. <u>Stay Positive and Expect the Best.</u> If we can remember to live from the point of view of the high self, all of these commandments will be natural and normal responses. Sometimes people get nervous when things go too well for too long. They think, "This is too good to be true. It can't last." My Huna teacher, Serge King, taught a way to solve this tendency. When things are

101

going great and you are afraid that it can't last, find a way to make it <u>even better</u>. Then you will be focusing your attention on improvement rather than failure.

7. <u>Go Within For All Answers.</u> The seventh commandment is one of the most important and that is to go <u>within</u> for all answers. As long as you stay in the limited conscious mind, you will be in the low self and will have limited answers.

When you go within, you go into your own inner sanctuary - the sacred place of your high self. Your high self sees, knows, and understands the whole picture, and can guide you according to your true purpose and goal in life.

8. <u>Do More of What You Love.</u> Only you know what lights your spirit the most; just do more of it. Ask yourself, "Is my heart really in it?" Nothing is worth doing unless your heart is in it. That doesn't mean that you have to quit your job, but it does mean that you will want to find ways to enjoy it more.

9. <u>Don't Let Anything Shake Your Power or Spirit.</u> The ninth commandment has to do with claiming your power and holding onto it. When did you start losing your power or spirit? Power and spirit are the same thing. Don't let any situation or person shake your power or spirit.

Your power is inside. When you go within, you find your power. If you gave it away, who did you give it to? What age were you? Where is it in your everyday life now? What do you do with it? Where does it go? Do you give it to your low self who then worries it away?

Do you look for answers outside yourself and give it to others? Make it a daily resolution not to let anything shake your spirit. Hold onto your power by standing in your own energy as you tap into the power within.

10. <u>Learn to Take Risks.</u> We need to start reclaiming ourselves and our magnificence, and stop pretending to be wimps. More than anything, we hate to take risks because it is scary and it means change. Change is our least favorite thing because it doesn't feel safe, but <u>healing means changing</u>.

CHAPTER TWENTY-EIGHT

Ascension

*Stop being so preoccupied
with death
and start living!*

The list of enlightenment definitions in the Appendix of this book, can serve as a guide for ascension. What is ascension? It is when you have so much joy and life within that you literally pop off the earth and go into another experience. It is easiest to do when there is a universal window. These windows appear during certain universal cycles, but one of the biggest ones in history will begin in 1997 and continue to stay open for about forty years.

The conditions for a universal birth (mass ascension) have been right since around 1993. We have not been able to experience this ascension because we haven't had enough joy and life in our bodies to do it. Once we learn to drop guilt and restore our inner power, we will achieve critical mass and will experience a mass ascension. The most likely date for this will be 2012 A.D., and it will be the grandest joy ride of all lifetimes. On the other side, we will each reach a destination that corresponds to our level of feeling and frequency. If we choose to live, we will begin a new life. If we choose to go back into the wholeness of Source, we will lose our individuality and go back into the whole.

We have arrived at the time in history that has been

talked about by the great prophets, sages, psychics, and religions for a very long time - not only the end of the 35,000 year cycle of the earth as a planet, but also the birth of a new universe. It is almost beyond comprehension, but it is true.

The work of all of us is to bring joy and life to the planet and into our lives. This is the work of all light workers. Unfortunately, many have become entrapped in serious schools of spirituality, and amidst the many rituals, rules, and partial truths, they have lost their light-heartedness.

For one thing, we have obsessed about death practically since the day we were born. Our parents and friends talk about it, the churches dwell on it, and we worry about dying almost every day of our lives. Philip says that each of us will think about death over one million times in our lifetime.

It doesn't seem apparent because much of the preoccupation is done on an unconscious level, but we really must begin to switch our focus to the process of living rather than dying.

There is no such thing as death. There is far too much literature proving that we exist after death to even question it anymore. It's time to relax and have fun and do the things you love. When you wake up in the morning, just ask yourself one question: "What can I do today that will bring joy into my life?", and then do it.

I have learned that it is helpful to ask everyday, "What does my body need? What does my mind need? What does my spirit need?" and then make sure those needs are met. I often suggest this to my clients, and it seems to contribute to their well-being and happiness.

Up until now, we have all been in a movie theater

participating in an illusion. We have taken it much too seriously, and it is time to change the movie to a more light-hearted comedy so that we can all laugh and have fun for a change. As characters in the movie, we can have fun creating the action, dialogue, and plot, and experience the exhilaration of our new creative efforts.

Ascension is about FEELING. It is about feeling life and joy. We can become <u>life</u> workers instead of light workers. This feeling of life is what has been missing in our understanding of ascension.

I once met a man named "Joybubbles" at a retreat. He was blind. He had chosen a name that made him feel good, and he literally bubbled with joy. When I changed my name to "Sunray," I experienced a major change in my perception of myself. All the past negative programming I had carried for so many years just seemed to disappear in the sunny energy of the new name. Today, I truly have a sunny personality.

What name would you choose? You might want to give yourself a name that reflects your most predominate positive feeling, or you might want to choose a name that has an energy that you makes you feel good. Every time your name is used, you associate with that energy. Every time I hear the name Paula Sunray, I absolutely love the sound and the feeling it gives me.

During these crucial times of the pre-birth period, it is important to find a passionate outlet in your life. What do you love passionately? Do lots of it. Find ways to release your intense feelings, because great intensities are beginning to flood the earth right now. You will need an outlet for them if you want to experience ease and comfort. Be careful to heed the warnings of your mind, body, and spirit, and keep your stress level as low as possible. Treat yourself gently and tenderly, listen to your needs and honor them, and have lots and lots of fun!

CHAPTER TWENTY-NINE

Our World is Insane

*You can either participate
in a world of insanity
or in a world of divinity.*

The Course in Miracles says that the world is insane. We can either concentrate on the world of insanity or the world of divinity. If we focus on the external world of insanity, we will experience stress, worry, anxiety, blame, anger, and guilt. If we focus on the inner world of divinity, we will experience peace and serenity.

The only sanity that we have in the world is the voice of the High Self. If we want to climb out of this insane world, we will need the help of the High Self.

The High Self will ask us to look at this world differently. In the <u>real</u> world, we are able to look beyond money, title, and good looks, to the sacred holiness within each and every person. In the real world, we heal our perceptions and base them on truth rather than illusion.

The root cause of all our problems is our belief system - the way we think. The outside world we experience is created by our beliefs and perceptions.

Self-esteem is a result of our belief system. When we identify with our High Self, we perceive ourselves to be holy children, and we feel our worth and divinity. It is impossible to have low self-esteem when we acknowledge our true divinity and worth as a high self.

Illness Is a Result of Our Perceptions

Metaphysics teaches us that we create our own reality, so therefore we must take responsibility for the illnesses we create. We don't blame ourselves, we simply recreate.

Very often, I see people struggling to heal sick bodies by trying to think positive thoughts, taking a variety of herbs and natural medicines, getting healings from body workers and hands-on healers, and doing inner visualizations, etc..

Why then do they not heal? I think it is because they are unpracticed manifestors in their daily life. They haven't been living consciously enough to create from conscious power. When they become ill, they suddenly try to become an expert in something they have practiced very little.

We can only create reality according to the maturity and expertise of our soul. We can have a mature soul when we change our perceptions to the sanity of the true inner world, and then activate those perceptions.

Many people are clear on their perceptions, they just don't know how to activate them. They must be willing and able to release their past wounds and come into present time where healing and health is.

Caroline Myss, a wonderful medical intuitive and teacher, is able to see illnesses in a person's body. According to her , we do not heal because we use our old past wounds for payoffs and to get intimacy.

Most people would be astounded at how much they use their wounds for payoffs in their life. Most people don't really want to heal. To heal means to change, and to change means to experience discomfort. Most people use their wounds as excuses to escape responsibility in life.

Caroline Myss says that we send our soul to wherever our thoughts are. If we think of the past, we send our soul to the past. Energy goes where attention goes. If the energy contains a message with it, it will then create the message.

If we concentrate on our wounds and identify with them, we are sending our soul to our wounded area and saying, "this is me." The soul then acts accordingly.

We will never be able to heal if we hang onto old wounds and hurts. We will begin to heal when we start identifying with life, joy, and forgiveness. When we send this type of vital force into our bodies, we are saying, "This is me," and we will heal.

Psychosomatic medicine has told us for years that we get sick because of our fearful thoughts, but it has never told us that we are ill as a result of our unwillingness to release old "garbage," and it has never told us how we can get well again.

STAYING IN THE NOW

We can only keep the past alive by actively thinking about it. If we send our energy to the past, it will not be available to use in the present. If we want to heal, we must have our life energy in the present. One of the reasons we are not better creators is that we are rarely in the present moment. If we want to create our own reality, we must focus our attention on the present moment.

Ms. Myss says that we can understand this concept

110

better by comparing it to our finances. If we use all of our money to finance our past, we won't have any money to finance our present. If we want to heal, we can no longer afford to send our energy to the past or the future.

CHAPTER THIRTY

Forgiveness

We must learn to forgive if we want to heal.

One of the reasons we have trouble forgiving is that we are very often focused on the past. We may try to forgive, but before we know it, we are in the past again in our mind, reliving the painful situation and reactivating the old pain. Once again, we are angry, hurt, and unforgiving.

Unforgiveness keeps us focused on the past, and since we are focused on the past, we have no energy in the present for our healing needs. Since forgiveness is one of the most powerful tools of recovery, we must learn to forgive if we want to heal.

Forgiveness results from the ability to move from the low self perception of victimhood to the high self ability to let go and create a healing.

Victim perception makes our reality negative, bitter, and angry. At some point in our evolution, we will have to take the old perception of revenge (which has been a data base in our biology for thousands of years), and dump it out of our systems. We will have to blow it out of our systems and replace it with a new program based on a higher truth.

It is a fallacy that we can be hurt or harmed by another individual. It is our own perceptions that are harmful; it is the perceptions of the low self which need to be addressed.

Victimhood disempowers you. Do you want to be a

fully empowered creator, or do you want to be a little lowly self who is filled with fear and hatred and has no power or life force?

Being attached to false perceptions weakens you. False perceptions are always attached to the past. If you could see your electromagnetic circuitry, you would see that most of the circuits are flowing into the past where you sit and lick your wounds. If you want to heal, you must place your circuitry in the present where the strength and healing life force is. Victims cannot heal. I repeat, <u>victims cannot heal.</u>

FORGIVENESS:HOW DO YOU DO IT?

So, if forgiveness is the single most powerful thing you can do for your own healing, how do you do it? First, you must release the idea that you have to accept the other person's words or actions. It is not necessary to condone the actions and deeds of the other person. In fact, you don't even have to "forget" in order to forgive. All you have to do is move to a higher level of perception and understanding. You can't solve low self problems at the level of the low self. You can only solve them from the point of view of the high self.

When you feel unforgiving, it really means that your needs and expectations didn't get met. You wanted something you didn't get. You will need to figure out what you were expecting and wanting, and then cancel the demands you were making from the low self.

What is it that you would have liked to have happened? What would you have preferred? You must be very clear on this before you go on to the next step.

When you cancel your demands and state your

preferences, you are in the act of forgiving. You are not dismissing the actions of the other person or even pardoning them. You are making a decision to suffer less inside. <u>You have decided not to punish yourself for what someone else did.</u>

As a creator, you can reassume the responsibility for your perceptions and actions, and allow others to be creators also. The Course in Miracles say that all people are either in a state of loving or in a state of <u>needing</u> love, and the only response that is needed on our part is to love back.

If someone hurts or injures us, they are crying out for love, and if we truly understand that, we will respond with love and not hate. The high self is the one who understands everyone's cry for love. We will never find it in the low self.

The only decision you will need to make is whether you want to put your energies into the low self or high self. Forgiveness is a high self perception, and it is a powerful and healing one. Which energy would you rather experience - a bitter and resentful one, or one of healing and peace? You are free to make the choice. No one will judge you or applaud you. Just remember to take the responsibility for your choice. It is never what another person does, it is how you respond that matters.

CHAPTER THIRTY-ONE

Miracles

Miracles happen every minute of every day.

Miracles are simply something you didn't expect. Miracles occur every minute of every day; you just need to be aware of them. Everything you experience on this planet is a miracle. Most people prefer to call them coincidences because they do not believe that miracles can be so common. To them, a miracle rarely happens, and it can only happen to a good and perfect person.

Many people miss the opportunity to rejoice in this life. So many times, they focus on what is wrong with the world and forget to see the incredible beauty and bravery around them.

The universe we live in is a supportive one, not a punishing one. It supports us in everything we do and think. It protects us, comforts us, and loves us. The evidence is everywhere.

How many times have you had a close call in an automobile and miraculously been saved? How many times have you been exposed to germs and illnesses and stayed well? How many times have you felt lost and alone and suddenly you felt a shift and felt better? How many times have you had a true crisis and your life was transformed as a result?

The beauty on this planet is a constant marvel. It is one of the most beautiful places in the universe and contains the rarest privileges and opportunities. Philip, my non-physical spiritual mentor, told me that the greatest sadness we will ever experience is when we die and understand for the first time what we missed. We never really understood the miracle of the physical body and the incredible magnificence of earth experience with its many flavors and subtleties. We were too afraid to take risks, and we never really allowed ourselves to do what we loved most. We never really <u>lived</u> life; we just existed. We missed so many opportunities and exercised so little courage.

Now is the time to resurrect our souls and our spirits, grab life by the tail, and let it take us for a magnificent ride! Now is the time to visit all the magic places - inner and outer. We can decide to experience all the flavors of our feelings and desires. We can touch our essence and glory in it, and we can touch the essence of others with our spirit and sacredness (remember that "sacred" is fun as well as serious and pensive).

Don't let the temporary outer disturbances of the earth fool you into thinking this is a dark and fearsome place. Nothing could be farther from the truth. It is what you make it. We are participating in the greatest miracle of all - the birth of a new and glorious universe. As a result of what we do together, it will either be a live birth or a still birth. It is for us to decide.

Please don't head for the nearest bomb shelter when things seem frightening. If all the frightened people go where they think it will be safe, it will then be unsafe because it is occupied by fearful people.

Just think "life." <u>Feel</u> life, and you will be safe. Choose to live, learn, and love, and you will be safe no matter where you are. When you are confident, joyful, and life-filled, that will <u>be</u> your experience. May you

116

truly experience the blessings of this time.

CHAPTER THIRTY-TWO

Growing Up

A master has no fear.

As a world filled with fear, our planet is filled with adults whose growth has been arrested at a young age. Most people do not like the hard work of growing up. There are very few mature adults on this planet.

There are certain telltale signs of maturity. As we grow up and mature, we become more open to new experiences and we stop trying to control others. As we begin to "grow up," we become more flexible and independent. We are also more forgiving and peaceful.

Maturity has nothing to do with chronological age. An older adult is not necessarily mature, whereas a younger person sometimes is. Our problems come when we expect older people to be wise and mature, especially our parents. Children are very often more mature than their parents.

Some adults who are fixated at a very early age are primitive and helpless and exhibit a lot of rage and fear. Others just want to be like everyone else. They don't like people who are different from themselves, and they believe in all sorts of rules. They follow church doctrine strictly and criticize those who do not.

Adults arrested at the child level are very competitive and they like to be winners. They do not look inside at their inner makeup; they are only interested in what is going on around them. They are also very concerned about how they look physically.

Most people never evolve past the level of adolescence. We have actually come to accept this as maturity. This is the level at which we explore religion and spirituality and are attracted to the arts and service fields. This level of person is a helper, a volunteer, a healer, or a counselor.

This "teen" adult likes alone time and values internal growth and freedom of expression. They are concerned about ecology, the rights of animals, and the rights of human beings. They are capable of lasting relationships, but they tend to rescue others and be overly concerned with other people's pain. They also project their problems onto others.

The true mature adult will allow others to find their own way and "let nature take care of nature." The true adult is more of a "be-er" than a "doer." They are positive in their attitude and don't react adversely when things don't go their way. They have many of the same characteristics as the adolescent, but they are able to stay emotionally detached from other people's problems. A true adult sees all of life's lessons from a high perspective and is able to learn lessons from every situation.

True adults look within for answers and don't look to others for authority. They don't care particularly about how they look. They like to play and have fun, and they are not workaholics. Adults choose work that they love whether it pays well or not. They like all types of people - rich and poor, young and old.

According to Jose Stevens in his book, Transforming Your Dragons, there are still more stages of maturation after the "adult" stage. As you can guess, there are not many people who achieve these higher levels.

The most mature and wise persons have no fear. Their concerns are for others, and they serve in a more quiet and powerful way. They are less focused on personal relationships and are more focused on their relationship with the whole.

"Master" level persons have rare and unusual abilities and are telepathic, insightful, and fear-free. They are not in a relationship because they are one with all, and they do not require a relationship to feel secure. They exude unconditional love and compassion, and they teach others to remember their God-hood and magnificence. They are the masters, avatars, and great spiritual leaders.

At the level of the high self, we are <u>all</u> master gods. We can achieve this level of living by releasing the fears of the low self, becoming personally aware, looking within for all answers, and loving ourselves and others unconditionally.

CHAPTER THIRTY-THREE

Making Decisions

Instead of letting life live you,
it is time to start living life.

You are constantly distributing your power. You are sending your spirit somewhere. You must be aware of where you are sending your spirit, otherwise you will lack power in your daily endeavors.

You have to <u>practice</u> using your power by making decisions. You have to consciously decide what you want to do with your spirit. Are you going to give your power to your ego or to your Spirit? The ego will try to control you through fear every time you try to make a decision. The Spirit will cheer you on and encourage you to move toward health and well-being.

When you make a decision, you will want to use your will and your power to consistently support yourself in that decision. You will want to give your energy and your power to Spirit so that you can accomplish the goal. It doesn't matter if the decision is right or wrong, it will affirm you by showing that you are capable of using your power to make a decision. If you don't like the results of your decision, use your power to make another one until you find exactly what you want.

People are unable to take risks because they don't have the power to support their decisions. The same is true in the struggle with addictions, etc. People give their power to the ego, which rules through fear, indecision, and struggle, rather than to the Spirit which lifts you above the level of fear and struggle and supports you with the powerful energy of love. It cheers you each step of the way.

When you make a decision, you must be able to state facts and state your emotions. You can then make an educated guess and support yourself with your decision. For example, you might have a herniated disc and your doctor recommends surgery. You are holistic in your beliefs and prefer to use hands-on healing. You also don't want to miss the two weeks of work that would be required if you had surgery.

First, look at the facts. The fact is that you are in pain and would like immediate relief. The second fact is, after consulting with several healers, you learn that hands-on-healing isn't usually as successful with herniated discs as surgery, and it can take some time before you get complete relief.

The second step is to be aware of your emotions and fears. Fear #1: "I may not get my raise if I take two weeks off work." Fear #2: "I'm afraid of being cut up and I don't like the idea of a scar on my body."

Now look at the facts and the fears, and make your best educated guess as to which would be best for you realistically. Process your fears, make your decision, and do it. If you talk to your boss and she says that you can rest at ease about your pay raise and that she understands the situation, you will now only have to deal with the scar. Will you be able to accept the fact that you will have a permanent scar? After talking with your doctor, you find out that the size of the scar will be minimal and after a year or so, it will be almost invisible. You now decide to have the surgery. This decision may be different from the one you would have made based on your fears and emotions only. You used the power of your Spirit to give you the courage to talk to your boss and your doctor, and as a result your fears were lessened.

This process can be used for other decisions as well, i.e., to stay in a relationship or not. Just state the facts, survey your emotions by writing them down, and then make your best educated guess.

Don't waver back and forth. Make a statement of power and make a decision, for better or worse. Sometimes a decision has to be based on the lesser of two "evils"- neither choice is exactly right, but one serves you better than the other.

Stop letting life live you, and start living according to your choices. Most people are severely disempowered and are unable to muster up enough power to stand up for their rights. The path of mastery is the path of empowerment. If you want to find your path, find the one that teaches you self-empowerment. Self-empowerment is making quick, decisive choices and following them through.

CHAPTER THIRTY-FOUR

Struggling With Your Inner Dragons

When you have become friends
with your inner dragons,
you have learned the true lessons of self-love.

In order to make decisions, we have to know who we are and then support who we are. We have to make friends with our inner fears by becoming aware of them. We could call these inner fears and insecurities our inner "dragons."

I have learned to bless the struggles in my life because it forces me to delve deeper into my inner psyche - into the inner shadows where my dragons live.

Whenever I feel angry or upset about something, I realize that I am feeling insecure about something. All of my struggles come from my own fears and insecurities. My struggles, then, are opportunities to become more aware of my inner dragons. The result is personal growth.

I have also become aware of the importance of understanding the dual nature of being both human and spirit. Most of our struggles come from this dual nature rather than the events which happen outside of ourselves.

As I have already stated, our insecurities come from the "low self." The low self is insecure and afraid of everything. It is very limited in its perceptions and has a very small vocabulary for resolving issues. This ego or low self mentality is a vicious circle - it can never find peace because of it's fear.

The other side of our dual nature, the high self, sees everything from a higher perspective and a different point of view. It knows and understands the nature of our struggles and sees them as opportunities for higher growth. The high self is the inner power system that leads us in the direction of our life purpose and soul growth. The low self sees the external world as the <u>only</u> world , and it exerts all of its energies to feed the world of illusion.

If we face our struggles from the point of view of the high self, we will have the courage and mental clarity to be aware of the inner dynamic that is causing our unhappiness. It will always be an insecurity of some kind, and by naming that insecurity, we will always realize that the outside problems are never the issue. The issue is our own insecurity.

In the old days, when something happened that I didn't like, I would numb up so that I wouldn't feel the pain, and I would quickly rationalize the problem so that I could blame someone else. Now, I pray for the courage to stay with the struggle so that I can find and name my inner dragons and make friends with them. I now find my inner dragons to be precious and adorable, and I realize that they were stirring up a little fuss so that I would pay attention to them and remember to love them like a mother loves her children.

Whenever there is a struggle, there is a lesson. One of the greatest lessons to be learned is to KNOW THYSELF. When we become aware of everything about ourselves, we have the opportunity to make peace with the dragons within.

When you become friends with your own precious dragons, you will have learned the true lessons of self-love and self-esteem. So I say to you, "Don't give up the struggle. Use your power to stay with them and let the friendship with your dragons build the bridge to peace and serenity. Then we can be bridge builders to each other and bridge builders to world peace."

Exercise For Working With Your Emotions

1. Breathe naturally and deeply for a few minutes.

2. Identify the specific part of your body that is feeling tight and closed off emotionally.

3. Imagine this emotion to be a little infant or inner child that is shut up within yourself.

4. Visualize yourself lifting the baby outside yourself and looking at it. Feel your love for it.

5. Ask it what it is feeling and what it has to say to you.

6. Listen carefully. Rock it, stroke it, and love it.

7. Tell this little infant that you will always be there to listen to it, comfort it, and love it, and then make sure that you keep your promise.

CHAPTER THIRTY-FIVE

Working With Your Inner Fears

Every time we have a negative reaction
to the outside world,
we must examine the <u>inner</u> cause
of this response.

There is no more important work than working with our inner fears. Our fears define us. They limit us and own us. We develop most of these fears at an early age and we continue to act them out for the rest of our lives unless we heal them.

Most people have a few major fears which dictate their inner responses and affect their relationship with themselves and others. Jose Stevens, in his book <u>Transforming Your Dragons</u>, names seven main groups of fears which he has observed in his clients over the years. He believes that these major fears are the cause of every dysfunction and addiction that we experience.

We must identify and work with these inner fears if we want to grow and evolve. Every time we have a negative reaction or response to the outside world, we must examine the inner cause of this response.

If children are given impossibly high standards when they are young, they will grow up with a <u>fear of vulnerability</u> and a <u>fear of being judged.</u> They will grow up trying to look good to other people. They want to be special in other people's eyes. Inside, they are self-conscious and shy, but outside they can seem smug and arrogant and self-important.

If children are constantly put down as youngsters, they will grow up with a <u>fear of being inadequate</u>. Because of their low self-esteem, they will apologize a lot and will lack confidence in themselves. On the inside, they will feel undeserving and will be self-condemning. On the outside, they will be meek, apologetic, and intimidated.

If children were incessantly told what to do without any choices, they will grow up with a <u>fear of authority</u>. They will grow up hard-headed and stubborn. On the inside, they will be inflexible and stuck, and on the outside, uncooperative and unbending.

If children are constantly forced to be obedient, they will eventually stop asserting themselves. They will grow up with the <u>fear of being trapped</u>. Inside, they will feel tormented and masochistic, and outside, they will be blaming and self-righteous. They are the classic victims who give up their needs and their rights.

Abused and abandoned children will grow up with the <u>fear of losing control</u>. They are often violent and wild. They are self-destructive. On the inside they feel out of control and hopeless, and on the outside they are reckless, violent, and addicted.

If children are abandoned and neglected, they will often grow up with the <u>fear of not having enough</u>. Their fear will often fixate on food, money, or sex. On the inside they will feel greedy, ravenous, and empty, and on the outside they will be selfish, possessive, and voracious.

When children are deprived of their own experiences, they will grow up with the <u>fear that there is not enough time</u>. This kind of person will rush through life with a great deal of stress and frenzy, and will try to do too much in too little time. Inside, they will be nervous and anxious, and outside, they will be short-tempered and intolerant.

Most of us fit into one or more of these categories. It will help us to look at these patterns and see how they run our lives. Personal growth involves taking control of one's life rather than letting these inner fears run the show. We can all learn to master these inner fears by recognizing them, loving them, and healing them. They are just like frightened little children who need our love and attention as well as our acceptance.

CHAPTER THIRTY-SIX

Relationships

When we relate to another person,
we are relating from an external place
or an internal one.

Our fears and insecurities are reflected in our relationships. In relationships, like everything else, we are dealing with the low self and high self. We could call them an "outer" self and an "inner" self. When we speak to and relate to another person, we are either acting and speaking from an external place or an internal one.

If we ask someone how they are feeling, they will usually respond with an "external" answer. If they are our mate, and we want to <u>really</u> know how they are feeling, we will want to receive an "internal" answer that comes from the deep true self.

Many couples content themselves with shallow, superficial interactions. It is not very fulfilling. If we want to retrieve the deep interaction with each other, we must learn to explore each other's deepest self and relate soul to soul.

Unfortunately, most people are so out of touch with their own integrity and inner self-awareness that they do not have the ability to relate from this deeper place. That is why self-work must always precede the beginning of a relationship. Both parties must have self-knowledge in order to co-author a journey of deep and meaningful interaction.

I have observed that many people do not make wise choices when they select a partner. Very often, mates are chosen from a deep insecurity and a fear of being alone. We want our mates to make us feel safe and secure; we want them to save us. In addition to doing personal growth work around these issues, we must consciously choose a mate well if we want to have a long term relationship of quality.

What are some of the things you should look for in a mate? Clarissa Pinkola Estes, Jungian analyst and storyteller, suggests the following:

1. Look at the map of their inner being first. Are they considerate, kind, and loyal? Are they tender and gentle with themselves? Are they able to care about you?

2. Look for someone who is flexible, curious, and wants to learn and grow.

3. Be sure to select someone who can weather the storms and stick it out.

4. Look for someone who is sensitive and capable of feeling and expressing their feelings and can be compassionate toward you when you are in pain. Look for someone who is strong enough to forgive.

5. You will want to select a partner who is able to respond from an honest place of truth and is content with who they are. Select someone who enjoys life and actively does things they love to do; they will

then be able to support you and not be threatened when you do the things you love.

6. Choose someone who is enough like you so that you have things to share together. When you have fun and rich experiences together, you build lovely memories which will act as glue for the relationship.

7. Select a partner who has similar principles and values as you. If you choose someone with similar values, it will lessen the potential conflict.

8. Be sure to find someone with a sense of humor and the ability to have fun. People who laugh together stay together.

9. Don't choose a partner with a deeply ingrained negative habit pattern like alcohol or drug use or abusive tendencies. It is unlikely they will overcome these tendencies. (Yes, it provides fertile ground for self-learning and self-growth, but it doesn't provide very stable ground for a good relationship.)

10. Pick someone who can stand on their own two feet so they won't lean into you for strength. Choose someone who really expands your life rather than diminishes it. A truly good mate will supplement your life with many treasures and gifts.

It is assumed that you, yourself, are able to provide all of the above for your partner. We cannot hold a partner very long if we are not able to live up to the very things we ask of the other person.

Once you choose a relationship, be prepared to do the hard work. Practice and learn skills of adaptability and compromise. Relationships require maintenance just like cars and houses so they won't depreciate in value. Be gentle and tender with each other, but be honest and stay in your own integrity.

The greatest art is the art of relationship, and when we co-create a life painting together, it can be the most beautiful art work of all.

CHAPTER THIRTY-SEVEN

Fear and Relationships

*Fear keeps us from leading meaningful lives
and having meaningful relationships.*

Our inner dragons of fear can keep us from having meaningful relationships. These fears can make us run from love and intimacy and hide from the very things we say we most want. Fear and relationship do not belong together.

Fear patterns begin early in life and affect every relationship we have. Jose Stevens, in his book Transforming Your Dragons, discusses these very fear patterns.

Dr. Stevens says the people who have great amounts of fear waste a lot of energy. They repeat the same mistakes over and over, and tend to see the world in black and white terms. They will see themselves as perfect or they will see themselves as worthless.

The fearful person moves away from her core self, living life in numbness. She lets other people dictate her life roles, and she carries great despair in the center of her being. She is only half-alive.

Neurotic fears wreak havoc in a relationship. A person who feels unworthy and unlovable will not make a good mate. A doormat person may say they love you, but it is just a sign of the need for approval and affection.

The type of person who has the fear pattern of

aggression does not trust people and protects himself by attacking first, before others can attack him. This type of person can lead a lonely life. When you are detached and aloof because of your vulnerability and fear of getting hurt, you can feel pretty lonely. You also distance relationships when you judge and criticize others.

Another fear pattern is when you are passive in a relationship. You never have to make a decision or take action. This is the pattern of low self-esteem.

Another type of inner fear pattern makes you act impatiently and intolerantly with others. In this way, you will quickly alienate and irritate other people.

Still another pattern, which we call the "victim," will blame you for everything and name you as the abuser. They will not take responsibility for their own actions, and they do not make good partners.

The kind of person who can never get enough, which is another fear dragon, will demand a lot in a relationship but give very little. And still another type, the person who fears control and abandonment, will be controlling themselves and will often have strong addictions.

The last type of fear pattern belongs to the person who hates authority and is rebellious and stubborn as a result. This stubbornness is difficult to deal with in a relationship.

All of us have some of these fears, so it is easy to see why relationships can be so difficult. It is fear that keeps us from leading meaningful and fulfilling lives, so the main work in our lives is confronting these fears and releasing and healing them.

CHAPTER THIRTY-EIGHT

Power and Relationships

Life is about relationship.
It is your main spiritual practice.

Relationships are difficult and challenging spiritual practices. They give us the opportunity to test our skills of communication, intimacy, authenticity, and integrity. They also give us a chance to retrieve our soul and our spirit.

Have you stopped dancing with your soul? Have you stopped letting your soul sing and express from its very heart and being? So many people have lost their song of life and their enchantment with life. When they learn to rekindle their heart song and reconnect with their life tune, they will be able to bring soul to a relationship. Two numb and lifeless souls do not create a very fulfilling relationship.

Everything we do in life is a relationship. We have a relationship with money, we have a relationship with our body, and we even have a relationship with our car. We have a relationship with everything!

As humans, we are all interdependent. True rewarding relationship is a union of two souls who connect from their life center - their spirit center. Staying in our own center and listening with our deepest inner knowing, is how we relate best.

The beauty of relationship is that it awakens the mystery and magic of our soul. We are like two gods creating amazing and wonderful universes of feelings and experiences together.

Why are these magical relationships so difficult to attain? For one, the element of trust is essential. We must arrive at a place where we trust ourselves and others. We must trust the fact that we know how to handle our life and make important decisions. We must also trust the fact that our mate knows how to do the same thing. Then, we can align our words and actions with our integrity, and expect the best. We must be reasonable in our expectations so that we don't place unreasonable demands on our partner.

Underneath it all, the only thing we all basically want is to be honored and respected exactly as we are. We want to feel safe, nurtured, and protected. We want to be validated, loved, and cherished. We also want to make our own choices and have those choices honored. We do not want to be told what to do or how to live our life.

A relationship is a mystery that is created stroke by stroke like a painting on a canvas. Each word we speak, every action we take, and each choice we make, is like a stroke on the canvas. Each day, we create a new segment of the painting, and each day, we add color, nuance, intensity, and energy. No two canvases are alike, just as no two people are alike.

Relationship is a miracle. It takes us all the way back to God who created us as companions. Every relationship we have is a reflection of the relationship we have with God. If we believe that God can love us, then we will believe that others can love us, and if we believe that we are not good enough for God to love, how will we be able to accept the love of others?

CHAPTER THIRTY-NINE

Personal Growth and Relationships

*The relationship of the future
will be a blend
of both the low and high selves.*

Let's face it. Most people are not growing very much. They have distanced themselves from being challenged and stretched. They are uncomfortable with change and are afraid to take risks. They protect their vulnerability at all costs, and are unwilling to do healing work. They want quick bandages, and they rush back to the world of stress and illusions and try to carve out some basic nutrition from a dead turkey.

The very evolution of our society shows the insecurity and fear of the people at large. Our relationships reflect our insecurities. The old relationships of the past have basically been an exchange of favors - the wife has exchanged sex for security and the husband exchanged work and being head of the household for a false sense of fulfillment. This is a marriage of two low selves, and this is the marriage of the average person.

The relationship of the future will be a blend of both the low self and high self. We will no longer have spouses and marriage certificates to make us feel safe; we will have partners who support our growth and encourage us to do what we love. We will have partners who encourage us to have our own power and express ourselves spontaneously and creatively.

This is the relationship of the future. It is the only one that will work. As soon as we have individuals who have reached that level of maturity, we will have relationships of quality and spirit. We will have true enlightenment. Enlightenment is self-actualization. When you are enlightened, the level of your success in life will depend upon your ability to let go of fear and insecurity and mistaken beliefs.

Enlightenment is not what you think. It is not about becoming something or gaining something. It is about giving up something . It is about losing or emptying; it is about emptying ourselves of our fears and our personal dragons.

We can achieve enlightenment by becoming personally aware. We can achieve it by peering into our inner core and looking at the shadows and the fears. Those little inner dragons are just unloved parts of ourselves. Once we find them and love them, we can tap into their vitality and energy, and use their power in our lives. When we bring them into our heart, they are no longer dragons; they are "spirit" entities who inspire us and lead us on our heroic journey of life. When we empty our low self of its fears and trepidation, there is room for God at our core. We must be empty to be filled, and when God fills us, we become enlightened.

CHAPTER FORTY

Enlightenment

Enlightenment is wherever you are.

Enlightenment is being aware and awake. Being "awake" means you are focused in the moment, and being "aware" means that you are <u>feeling</u> the experience of the moment. Enlightenment requires both of these. When you are awake and aware, you are focused in physical reality and spiritual reality at the same time.

Being asleep is a function of the low self. It means going through life mechanically without awareness. It means that you don't know who you are and you don't know where you are going.

It is very difficult, if not impossible, to be in a continual state of enlightenment on the physical plane. It is best to think of enlightenment as moments and periods of time when we are living congruently out of both our high self and low self at the same time. That is to say, we are running our low self with high self consciousness. We are living life from our higher centers.

You can find enlightenment and you can lose it. It is both a conscious and unconscious experience. We must consciously be aware and awake, and yet there are moments when bliss just flows through us like a breeze that came from within, blowing through our being like the breath of God.

God <u>does</u> breathe through us when we are open,

relaxed and safe, and our mind and body are so calm that our spirit can be fully present.

Most people seem to think of enlightenment as something to work toward or achieve in the future. If you think of enlightenment as something you haven't reached, then you won't be connecting with it in the present moment.

Enlightenment is not removing yourself from the physical plane. It is integrating higher consciousness into the present physical moment. Enlightenment can be seen as a place you can visit in the present moment and not a place to work toward in some future moment.

Spiritual achievement is always best seen within the context of your everyday situation. Spirituality is LIFE, and every bit of life is spirituality. The more one wants to escape from this life, the more one is out of touch with the true soul purpose in this lifetime. The sooner one begins to love every aspect of this life, the sooner one will be birthed into their true Self.

Universal Mind Meditation

1. Relax your body. Breathe out all tension and stress. Breathe in peace and safety.

2. Visualize a flow of energy from your tailbone to deep within the earth. Ground and anchor yourself into the earth.

3. Let a flow of energy move from your heart and spread outward like the rays from the sun until those rays fill the whole universe.

4. Go deep within and feel the breathe of the Divine Spiritual Source flowing throughout your whole being. You are One with the All. You are Universal Mind, omnipresent and all knowing. Let the wisdom and knowledge of the Universal mind teach you and tell you what you need to know.

5. Feel the Spirit of this Universal Source and let yourself be healed in the flowing breath of this Spirit. Feel the healing energy of this breath as it flows throughout your physical body, healing whatever needs to be healed. Let the breath of healing flow throughout your mind and emotions, healing old painful issues. Release them with the out breath.

6. Let the breath breathe you and heal you. Let the breath meditate you. Let the breath begin to move you on your path. Let go and surrender and let it move you. The Universal Mind and Breath will always take you where you need to go according to your own Divine Plan. Just relinquish control and know that all is in divine order. Let yourself be moved. Let go of your need to control. That is the way of the master and you are a master.

CHAPTER FORTY-ONE

The Principled Life

Enlightenment is letting go of the things
that don't serve you.
It is leading a principled life.

We flow best with Universal Spirit when we lighten our baggage and stop trying to play all the games of mass consciousness. If we dump all those games and align ourselves with our principles, we will live an elegant and graceful life. When we live a principled life, we are aware of our values and we honor our values in all that we do. We are aware of the triune aspect of ourselves and we honor our mind, body, and spirit.

When my clients complain that something doesn't feel right in their life, I remind them that they really have three parts and each part must be taken care of individually. When all three parts are happy, then their life will be happy. These three parts are mind, body, and spirit. I suggest to each of you that every morning you tune in with your body and ask it what it needs. Make sure that at sometime during the day you will meet that need so that the body will feel satisfied and content. Do the same for the mind and the spirit and honor their needs also. It is important to identify which part of yourself is miserable or unhappy, listen to it, and give it what it needs. This is what makes a happy life.

To lead a principled life, you have to study the things that <u>own</u> you - the things that have power over you. Just ask yourself "What is it that I cannot live without?"

The answers will be the things that own you and have power over you. Some of the things that cause you to lose your power are drugs, fear, negative habits, food, and sex. It is time to stop acting like a little weakling and start taking control of your life. Regain your power by learning to say "no" to destructive patterns. As Caroline Myss says, "Stop imitating ordinary mortals and start playing hardball." You have been a wimp long enough. Confront yourself, start shaping up, and stop making excuses. In the world that is coming, you will need to be strong, commanding, and powerful. Start practicing now!

This doesn't mean that you can't be kind and gentle with yourself. In fact, that is the next step. You have been criticizing and terrorizing yourself long enough with your judgments and fears. It is time to take a new tact. Care enough about yourself so that you start supporting yourself with wise choices for your mind, body, and spirit. Let this kindness flow into your relationships also. Stop criticizing, and start honoring others exactly as they are. Apply your principles in your relationships. Relationships are gifts entrusted to us to handle with reverence and care. Ask yourself how you would like to be treated and return the same favor.

In the new world to come, we will also stop supporting each other's dysfunction, and we will learn to be honest when asked. When we honor our own personal integrity, we are truthful in all that we do. We no longer treat others like little weaklings who can't take care of themselves, we don't couch our words in cotton to save someone else's feelings, and we report what we think and see from an objective point of view that is not colored with emotion and defensiveness. Learning to be objective is part of the principled life.

We are addicted to our old patterns and they will no longer serve us. The greatest addiction we have is our negative thoughts. It is the greatest disease on our planet and could be thought of as a plague. Since our thoughts are our greatest power, we must practice regular "thought" checkups, and find ways to heal our negativity.

We must heal our addiction to violence, turn off the TV, and stop reading the newspaper. Addictions create, just like thoughts do. We create whatever we focus on.

Be clear about what you believe and don't believe, and don't accept the beliefs of others if they don't correspond with your belief system. Go deep within your heart and be clear about your beliefs. Which ones are really yours and which ones came from your parents, school, church, government, and past habits? You cannot have spiritual principles unless you can define your own beliefs and values.

The greatest work is the release of your fears. All the troubles on this earth have been a result of fear and insecurity. If we could each drop our own fears and insecurities, we would put an end to the chain of cause and effect, and create a world of harmony and peace.

Those days are coming. You will be given a chance to choose two future worlds: one based on the zest and optimism of valued life, and the other based on panic and fear. It is truly your choice. You are in the process right now of creating your future and the future of the world.

CHAPTER FORTY-TWO

Self-Actualization: Spirit and Power

You must learn how to discipline your spirit.

If truth be known, we are not meant to sit around in some enlightened state; we are here to become self-actualized and healed. We are meant to gather our power and energy, strike out on our own, leave the prison walls of religious and societal rules, and think for ourselves.

At some point, we must leave the falseness of the systems which dictate our behavior and beliefs, and begin a journey which will take us to the truth within. When the "I" is birthed within us, the real journey begins.

The low self has to belong to a group to feel safe. It needs the validation and approval of the group to feel okay about itself. It lets the group make all the decisions.

The true self can only be found when we leave the group structure and look within for answers. We have to "unplug" ourselves from the outside power system and plug into the inner one. We have to reclaim who we are and make our own decisions based on our own integrity and authenticity.

To become self-actualized, we will need to examine the fears of the low self and heal them. We will need to define what frightens us most and then allow ourselves to walk right into the center of that fear and find out how it got there and what it has to tell us.

The object is not to kill off our fears; it is to listen to them, support them, and affirm them. They are our inner children. They are frightened and lonely and just want to be acknowledged, heard, and comforted. That is our only job - to be a loving parent to our inner feelings, and to love and accept them just as they are.

To become self-actualized, we have to summon up our courage, beef up our muscles, take some risks, and do some hard work. In many ways, people live wimpy lives. They have gotten lazy and do not want to exert the effort to heal and change. They do a lot of complaining but very little to change things for the better.

People have forgotten how beautiful and precious they are. They have received very little authentic instruction as to how to develop their spirituality. Our religions have kept secrets in order to control and manipulate us, and we have little by little been removed from our true inner power.

External instruction and dogma can never lead us where we want to go. Something will always be missing. We can only find the missing links within our own God-hood. The only valuable teachings are those which help us learn how to access the deep well of inner wisdom which runs through our being like an endless river.

We must also take our hands off the steering wheel of our life and stop trying to control everything. We need to pray for the guts to follow our own inner spirit and drive our life from our own integrity and principles. The need to control comes from fear, and fear is a sign that we have lost touch with our own guidance.

At some point, each of us has to take the plunge and learn to trust ourselves and the universe. We must integrate our mind and our heart because they are the parents of all creations. A single parent can't handle an unruly child.

Our willpower needs strong healthy parents who are firmly in control, otherwise we will never learn to handle our addictions and powerlessness. We must use both our mind and our heart to make caring choices for how we treat ourselves and our bodies, and we must consult with both of them when we make important decisions in our lives.

SPIRIT AND POWER

We have to learn to discipline our spirit. It has been out of control for a long time. We must be very careful how we use our spirit and very careful where we send it. If we continually send it to the past, it will not be with us in the present. If we are not consciously in charge of our spirit, it will become unruly and go where it wants to go.

The process of learning how to keep our spirit present is a difficult one. Every thought we think and every word we say is a command to our spirit. If we want to enjoy good physical health, we will want to keep our spirit here in the present moment because it is our spirit which is the vital force that runs through our body. Our spirit is the "prana" (the breath of God), that feeds and nourishes our cells and all parts of our body.

Our spirit must be present in order for us to be empowered and in order for us to create our reality. The reason most people are impotent when they try to create what they want, is that their spirit is plugged into their fears, wounds, and past experiences, and is not present in the moment, where it is needed for creation. The key to everything in our lives is how we use our energy and how we use our power. We cannot create or heal until we have learned how to structure our energy and use our power effectively.

CHAPTER FORTY-THREE

Your Life Purpose

Your life purpose is to <u>live</u> life rather than just to survive. You are just beginning to <u>feel</u> life. Do the things you love, have fun, feel everything passionately, and you will have achieved your life purpose. Purpose is not an action, it is a feeling.

I was recently working with a client in a private counseling session, and every time I would say something, she would whip out her notebook and furiously record everything I said. At the end of the session she said to me, "What should I be doing and practicing?"

I thought for a moment, trying to sum up the wisdom of a lifetime, and I said to her, "Nancy, just live. Just live. Live and express. Feel and express. <u>Feel</u> as you breathe in, and <u>express</u> as you breathe out. Feel the life force in all that you do, and you will have done what you came to do."

I continued, "There is nothing to learn, nothing to memorize, nothing to practice. There is just being and feeling. God is a FEELING and not a thing. The only way to connect with Source is through feeling."

I then had her sit for a few minutes and feel LIFE in her body - in every cell and fiber of her being. I had her breathe in life from all around her, and then breathe out, filling herself with this life force so that it spread and vibrated throughout her whole being.

After a few minutes I asked her how she was feeling. She opened her eyes, looked at me ecstatically, and said, "I feel such life and joy that I want to dance. I feel wonderful!"

I then suggested that if she were to maintain this feeling on a regular basis, she would be giving the earth and everybody around her the gift of life and healing. All she had to do was BE this energy and not DO a thing.

She went away a happy woman. She felt relieved that she didn't have to meditate an hour a day, study some complicated course, or perform fancy rituals. She finally understood her life purpose.

My beloved friend, Philip, says that we came here with one purpose and that is to be excited about living, to be ourselves, and to have fun. He told me that the average life span is seventy years, and during that time, the average person really only "lives" and experiences TRUE LIFE ENERGY for a total of about 20 minutes.

Life is excitement, enthusiasm, passion. Joseph Campbell was right on when he said "follow your bliss." Our planet has very little life and joy. We may hear a lot of talk about ascension these days, but most people do not have enough joy and life to ascend.

Speaking for myself, I have begun to let my inner child play more. I blow bubbles, play little games, sing little songs, dance little dances, and look at the stars. I have stars that glow in the dark all over my bedroom, so when I fall asleep at night, I am floating amidst a twinkling and friendly universe. I wake up very happy.

I also bought a little parcel of land surrounded by birch trees and pine trees where the birds sing and the deer feed. I am learning to relax and give up the frantic search for enlightenment. I now know that enlightenment is how I feel <u>now</u> and is not something far off in the distance that I have to strive for or deserve. It is wherever I am when I am feeling life and joy and peace.

Everyday, I am getting better at sustaining this feeling, and everyday, I am making more and more choices to give up fear and just live life at its fullest. I'm making fewer judgments, I'm less critical of myself, and I'm enjoying each and every day in a more spontaneous way.

We are all living at a time in history that promises to be the most exciting time we have ever experienced on this earth plane. We are in the process of experiencing a new birth - the birth of a new universe and the birth of new bodies. Our new bodies will be fed and run on the energy of life and joy. The sooner we start the feeding process, the better. We can all help the birth in this way.

Thank you for reading this book. I hope it has inspired you in a helpful way.

Love,

Paula

In Closing

In the months since the book was first written, I have thought of a few closing comments I would like to make. We are crossing time and space into a New Millennium. You have the choice of taking the ride with your High Self in the front seat with you or the Low Self. You will create everything in your life according to the choice you make.

Many of you are mapmakers and dreamweavers for the future. That means that you chose to be here at this time to hold and create a positive future for the world, no matter what is going on around you.

The only school that exists is LIFE itself. One of the ways to create a positive future is to live a positive life today. Learn to live life with gusto and enthusiasm. If you don't take the time to enjoy life today, you are missing the whole point of why you are here.

Since every thought, word, and deed creates an energy, that energy becomes the gift you give to the world. The highest form of service to the planet, then, would be the highest form of energy which is PLAY, FUN, and HUMOR.

The most dangerous human being at this time is not the dictator or the terrorist, it is the individual who sits back and waits for the world to cave in and feels incapable and powerless to do anything about it.

Each and every individual affects the entire world with each choice, each decision, and each thought they make. The energy of your choice is the most powerful tool you have.

I invite you to take a moment or two each day to envision the world as a bright and glorious place, and to plan each day so that you create as much magic and joy as possible.

In this time of the Great Shift, you and your body have been reprogrammed with incredible spiritual energy. You are now a magical being with magical powers, and how you use those powers will determine the destiny of the world, much like a ripple in a pond. It is time to do what you came to do. It is time to wake up and remember who are you--a full creator-god. Have fun and create the most glorious world possible-- for yourself and for the universe.

Appendix

What is Enlightenment?

1. Enlightenment is living without fear.
2. Enlightenment is remembering to laugh when life is the most serious.
3. Enlightenment is letting go of things that no longer serve you.
4. Enlightenment is leading a principled life.
5. Enlightenment is <u>feeling</u> and not <u>thinking</u>.
6. Enlightenment is staying in the moment.
7. Enlightenment is dropping your illusions.
8. Enlightenment is being open to change and taking risks.
9. Enlightenment is seeing challenges as opportunities rather than punishments.
10. Enlightenment is experiencing life and not just living it.
11. Enlightenment is looking at your shadows and loving them.
12. Enlightenment is <u>being</u> and not <u>doing</u>.
13. There is no such thing as enlightenment. There is only process.
14. Enlightenment is remembering who you are.
15. Enlightenment is expressing your true inner self.
16. Enlightenment is the joining of the low self and high self in an abiding love.
17. Enlightenment is keeping your own inner lamp lit when everything else is dark.
18. Enlightenment is realizing that everyone else is a reflection of yourself, and that everyone else is a part of you.

19. Enlightenment is making God laugh.
20. Enlightenment is knowing that life is a river that takes you where you need to go.
21. Enlightenment is integrating and healing your fears.
22. Enlightenment is being responsible for your own reality.
23. Enlightenment is awareness.
24. Enlightenment is knowing that your fears and insecurities cause your suffering.
25. Enlightenment is understanding that life is expression and not repression.
26. Enlightenment is understanding that what you have learned so far is not necessarily true.
27. Enlightenment is knowing that NOW is the only moment that counts.
28. Enlightenment is realizing that you cannot love what you are afraid of.
29. Enlightenment is realizing that when you do nothing you are allowing the past to continue.
30. Enlightenment is understanding that whatever you give out, you will receive in return.
31. Enlightenment is knowing that everything you need in life is inside of you.
32. Enlightenment is being who you were to start with.
33. Enlightenment is understanding that difficult people and difficult situations are your teachers in life and help you grow.
34. Enlightenment is understanding that most things in life are not important. Isolate the few things that are important and focus on them.
35. Enlightenment is knowing that this is a supportive universe and not a punishing one.

36. Enlightenment is realizing that you can't be happy unless you know what you want.
37. Enlightenment is knowing the difference between wants and needs. ("Wants" are the little daily things that are supplemental to your life and are temporary in nature, and "needs" are the requirements of your true inner self in order to have quality and meaning in your life.)
38. Enlightenment is understanding that you build your own fences. The universe can only fill your life as far as the fences allow.
39. Enlightenment is knowing that if there is something in your life you don't like, you can change it.
40. Enlightenment is questioning the old systems and following your own truth.
41. Enlightenment is knowing that you are the only authority in your life.
42. Enlightenment is letting go of your need for approval and the need to control.
43. Enlightenment is knowing that if it is "simple" it is powerful and if it is "joyful" it is spiritual.
44. Now make a list of your own definitions of enlightenment.

Enlightenment Cards

Dr. Sunray has created special Enlightenment Cards to use on a daily basis for spiritual transformation. These 42 enlightenment cards and companion booklet are for those who would like to focus on their spirituality on a daily basis and accomplish one important spiritual goal per day. These cards are the ultimate tool for life mastery.

To order your cards, send a check for $29.95 to the National Interfaith Seminary, 2144 Jefferson Avenue, St. Paul, MN 55105 or call 651 690-4632. You may also use a credit card by calling 1 800 752-3691.

RECOMMENDED BOOKS

Transforming Your Dragons by Jose Stevens. Bear
    and Company, 1994.
You Can Heal Your Life by Louise Hay. Hay
    House, 1984.
Learning To Love Yourself by Gay Hendricks.
    Prentice Hall Press, 1990.
Conversations With God by Neale Donald Walsch.
    G.P. Putnam's Sons, 1996.
Love is Letting Go of Fear by Gerald Jampolsky.
    Bantam Books, 1989.
Anatomy of the Spirit by Caroline Myss. Harmony
    Books, 1996.
Understanding: Eliminating Stress and Dissatisfaction In
Life and Relationships by Jane Nelsen. Sunrise Press,
    1986.
Heart Thoughts by Louise Hay. Hay House, 1990.
Why People Don't Heal and How They Can by
    Caroline Myss. Harmony Books, 1997.
The Power of Self-Love: How to Build Your Self-
Esteem by Dr. Paula Sunray. Sunray Healing Haven,
    1995.
Metaphysics Made Easy by Dr. Paula Sunray. Sunray
    Healing Haven, 1993.
I Come as a Brother by Bartholomew. High Mesa
    Press, 1986.
The Resilient Self by Steven and Sybil Wolin. Villard
    Books, 1993.
Passion To Heal by Echo Bodine. Nataraj
    Publishing, 1993.

Neurosis is a Painful Style of Living by Samuel
    Greenberg. Signet Books, 1971.
Man's Search For Meaning by Viktor Frankl. Pocket
    Books, 1939.
Unconditional Love and Forgiveness by Edith
    Stauffer. Triangle Publishers, 1987.
Feeling Good: The New Mood Therapy by David
    Burns. Signet Books, 1980.
The Power of Your Subconscious Mind by Dr.
    Joseph Murphy. Prentice Hall, 1963.
Finding Joy by Charlotte Kasl. Harper Perennial,
    1994.
Joy Riding the Universe by Sheradon Bryce.
    Homewords Publishing, 1993.
The Sirius Connection by Lazaris. NPN Publishing,
    1996.
Ultimate Journey by Robert Monroe. Doubleday,
    1994.
A Return to Love by Marianne Williamson.
    HarperPerennial, 1992.

SPIRITUAL COUNSELING COURSE

The National Interfaith Seminary, directed by Dr. Paula Sunray, offers an outstanding 26 week training course for spiritual counselors. This course ordains you as a Minister of Spiritual Counseling and covers the following subjects: (Call 651-690-4632 for more information).

An Overview of Counseling and Psychotherapy
Personality Theory
Neurosis versus Healthy Living
The Transformational Therapist
Principles of Full Living
Your High Self/ Intuition
Building Your Self-Esteem and Confidence
Inner Child Work
Self-Healing as a Counselor
Shame and Guilt
Feelings and Emotions
Forgiveness
Why People Don't Heal
Transforming Your Dragons
Stages of Spirituality and Maturity
Relationships
Boundaries
Chakra Therapy and Totem Psychology
Recycling Fear and Negativity
The Hero's Journey
The Basic Skills of Spiritual Counseling
Your Mission in Life
The Counseling Practice

SPIRITUAL HOME STUDIES PROGRAMS

The National Interfaith Seminary and Higher Learning Center for Esoteric and Metaphysical Studies,, directed by Dr. Paula Sunray, offers many spiritual home study courses: Minister of Spiritual Studies, Minister of Healing, Minister of Spiritual Counseling, Honorary Doctor of Divinity, Doctor of Metaphysics, Mastery Level Classes, Personal Cosmology, Master Practitioner of Advanced Energy Medicine, Ph.D. in Religion, Shamanism, In-Depth Psychic Awareness, and New Millennium Studies.

To inquire about spiritual home study courses and ordinations, call 1-800-752-3691 or write National Interfaith Seminary, 2144 Jefferson Avenue, St. Paul, MN 55105. Fax 651 690-5021.

OTHER BOOKS BY DR. PAULA SUNRAY

Metaphysics Made Easy. This 120 page book covers practically every subject of metaphysics. It is easy to read with summaries at the end of each chapter. Cost $9.95 plus $3.00 postage.

The Enchanted Garden: Seven Stepping Stones For Recovery. This book is for the person in recovery in the style of the 12 step program. Cost $4.95 plus $1.25 postage.

The Power of Self-Love: How to Build Your Self-Esteem. This precious book helps you to understand the art of loving and accepting yourself exactly as you are. You will learn how to turn off your critical inner voice and examine the dynamics of glowing self-worth. A self-esteem quiz is included. Cost $3.95 plus $1.00 postage.

To order the books above, send your check to National Interfaith Seminary, 2144 Jefferson Avenue, St. Paul, MN 55105 or call 651-690-4632.

WORLD WIDE WEB SITE

To study our programs in depth, visit our world wide web site at: **http://spiritual-home-study.com** or send an E-mail to **pvsun@aol.com**

Dr. Paula Sunray has been teaching classes on personal growth and metaphysical spirituality for 17 years. She is director of the Sunray Healing Haven and National Interfaith Seminary in St. Paul, Minnesota, where she trains and teaches healers, ministers, counselors, and spiritual students in addition to maintaining her own private practice. Dr. Sunray is a leading expert in the field of mind-body-spirit transformation and is a frequent lecturer, workshop leader, educator, and inspirer to many.

Petals of Life Order Form

Order Additional Copies of *Life Skills for The New Millennium*

Ordering options available:

1. **Simply return to <http://www.petalsoflife.com> to order as a download, book on disk, or print version. We accept virtual checks and credit cards.**
2. **Please print and fill in the order form on this page to pay by regular check or credit card.**

Mail Your Order To:

**Petals of Life
231-C Oil Well Road
Jackson, TN 38305**

Name:_____

Address:_____

City, State, Zip:_____

# of E-books (PDF) as downloads _____ **@ $3.00 each** _____

E-Mail address(es) to send book to:_____

# of E-Books on Disk (PDF) _____ **@ $6.50 each =**_____
(ISBN 1-892745-21-6)

# of Printed Books _____ **@ $17.95 each =** _____
ISBN 1-892745-22-4

(above charges include shipping and handling)

Total = $ _____

Credit Card #_____

Name on Card:_____

Expiration Date:_____

Authorized Signature:_____

Thank You For Your Order!

Other Books Available From Petals of Life
Order Direct From The Publisher
http://www.petalsoflife.com

Alternatives: An Internet Guide
by Michele J. Johnson
ISBN: 1-892745-04-6
Format: Book on Disk or Download

Over 400 of the best web sites about natural health & healing, alternative
solutions and therapies. This is a must-have book for anyone interested in
the field of alternative therapy and healing! Alternatives: An Internet Guide
is by far the best reference tool on the internet today! Everyone interested in
this field can benefit, including students, therapists, and anyone looking for
new ways and methods of healing.

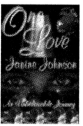

One Love by Janine Johnson
ISBN - E-Book(PDF)-1-892745-12-7
Print - 1-892745-11-9

A "healing fiction" novel teaching about unconditional love in a unique
way. An unbelievable tale, filled with mystical adventure and deep wisdom,
containing the power to uncover the unconditional love in your heart,
encouraging you to offer that love to yourself and others, making your world
a better place to live.